Computer Science, Technology and Applications

Computer Science, Technology and Applications

Information and Knowledge Systems
Manaswini Pradhan, PhD (Editor)
Satchidananda Dehurl (Editor)
2023. ISBN: 979-8-89113-303-7 (Softcover)
2023. ISBN: 979-8-89113-390-7 (eBook)

Emerging Applications of Blockchain Technology
Vinod Kumar Shukla, PhD (Editor)
Sonali Vyas, PhD (Editor)
Shaurya Gupta, PhD (Editor)
Suchi Dubey, PhD (Editor)
2023. ISBN: 979-8-89113-101-9 (Hardcover)
2023. ISBN: 979-8-89113-185-9 (eBook)

Digital Transformation – Modernization and Optimization of Wireless Networks
Ram Krishan, PhD (Editor)
Manpreet Kaur, PhD (Editor)
Jagtar Singh, PhD (Editor)
Shilpa Mehta, PhD (Editor)
Vikas Goyal (Editor)
2023. ISBN: 979-8-89113-042-5 (Softcover)
2023. ISBN: 979-8-89113-116-3 (eBook)

Digital Twins: The Industry 4.0 Use Cases: The Technologies, Tools, Platforms and Application
Kavita Saini, PhD (Editor)
Pethuru Raj Chelliah, PhD (Editor)
2023. ISBN: 979-8-89113-057-9 (eBook)

More information about this series can be found at
https://novapublishers.com/product-category/series/computer-science-technology-and-applications/

Lottie Gould
Editor

Digital Identification

Privacy, Security and Technology

Copyright © 2024 by Nova Science Publishers, Inc.

All rights reserved. No part of this book may be reproduced, stored in a retrieval system or transmitted in any form or by any means: electronic, electrostatic, magnetic, tape, mechanical photocopying, recording or otherwise without the written permission of the Publisher.

We have partnered with Copyright Clearance Center to make it easy for you to obtain permissions to reuse content from this publication. Please visit copyright.com and search by Title, ISBN, or ISSN.

For further questions about using the service on copyright.com, please contact:

	Copyright Clearance Center	
Phone: +1-(978) 750-8400	Fax: +1-(978) 750-4470	E-mail: info@copyright.com

NOTICE TO THE READER

The Publisher has taken reasonable care in the preparation of this book but makes no expressed or implied warranty of any kind and assumes no responsibility for any errors or omissions. No liability is assumed for incidental or consequential damages in connection with or arising out of information contained in this book. The Publisher shall not be liable for any special, consequential, or exemplary damages resulting, in whole or in part, from the readers' use of, or reliance upon, this material. Any parts of this book based on government reports are so indicated and copyright is claimed for those parts to the extent applicable to compilations of such works.

Independent verification should be sought for any data, advice or recommendations contained in this book. In addition, no responsibility is assumed by the Publisher for any injury and/or damage to persons or property arising from any methods, products, instructions, ideas or otherwise contained in this publication.

This publication is designed to provide accurate and authoritative information with regards to the subject matter covered herein. It is sold with the clear understanding that the Publisher is not engaged in rendering legal or any other professional services. If legal or any other expert assistance is required, the services of a competent person should be sought. FROM A DECLARATION OF PARTICIPANTS JOINTLY ADOPTED BY A COMMITTEE OF THE AMERICAN BAR ASSOCIATION AND A COMMITTEE OF PUBLISHERS.

Library of Congress Cataloging-in-Publication Data

ISBN: 979-8-89113-494-2

Published by Nova Science Publishers, Inc. † New York

Contents

Preface		vii
Chapter 1	**I Am Who I Say I Am: Verifying Identity While Preserving Privacy in the Digital Age**	1
	House Committee on Financial Services	
Chapter 2	**Promoting Digital Privacy Technologies Act**	129
	The Committee on Science, Space, and Technology	
Chapter 3	**Deep Fakes and National Security**	163
	Kelley M. Sayler and Laurie A. Harris	
Chapter 4	**Science and Tech Spotlight: Deepfakes**	169
	United States Government Accountability Office	
Chapter 5	**Deepfake Task Force Act**	177
	Committee on Homeland Security and Governmental Affairs	
Index		183

Preface

This book explores how to leverage the power of artificial intelligence (AI) to create a secure digital identity, and how to leverage those capabilities with digital infrastructure, such as mobile ID, to make internet access safer, more available, and more equitable for everyone. Digital identification is a long-overdue and necessary tool for the U.S. economy to transition into the digital age, while preventing fraud, ensuring privacy, and improving equity.

Chapter 1

I Am Who I Say I Am: Verifying Identity While Preserving Privacy in the Digital Age[*]

House Committee on Financial Services

Friday, July 16, 2021
U.S. House of Representatives,
Task Force on Artificial Intelligence,
Committee on Financial Services,
Washington, D.C.

The task force met, pursuant to notice, at 12 p.m., via Webex, Hon. Bill Foster [chairman of the task force] presiding.

Members present: Representatives Foster, Casten, Adams, Garcia of Texas, Auchincloss; Gonzalez of Ohio, Budd, and Taylor.

Ex officio present: Representative Waters.

Chairman FOSTER. The Task Force on Artificial Intelligence will now come to order.

Without objection, the Chair is authorized to declare a recess of the task force at any time. Also, without objection, members of the full Financial Services Committee who are not members of the task force are authorized to participate in today's hearing.

As a reminder, I ask all Members to keep themselves muted when they are not being recognized by the Chair. The staff has been instructed not to

---

[*] This is an edited, reformatted and augmented version of Virtual Hearing before the Task Force on Artificial Intelligence, of the Committee on Financial Services, U.S. House of Representatives, One Hundred Seventeenth Congress, First Session, Serial No. 117–39, dated July 16, 2021.

In: Digital Identification
Editor: Lottie Gould
ISBN: 979-8-89113-494-2
© 2024 Nova Science Publishers, Inc.

mute Members, except when a Member is not being recognized by the Chair and there is inadvertent background noise.

Members are also reminded that they may participate in only one remote proceeding at a time. If you are participating today, please keep your camera on. And if you choose to attend a different remote proceeding, please turn your camera off.

Today's hearing is entitled, "I Am Who I Say I Am: Verifying Identity While Preserving Privacy in the Digital Age."

I now recognize myself for 4 minutes to give an opening statement.

Today, we are here to explore how we can leverage the power of artificial intelligence (AI) to create a secure digital identity, and how we can leverage those capabilities with digital infrastructure, such as mobile ID, to make internet access safer, more available, and more equitable for all of us. Digital identification is a long-overdue and necessary tool for the U.S. economy to transition into the digital age, while preventing fraud, ensuring privacy, and improving equity.

Especially since COVID, we find ourselves increasingly working, transacting, and interacting online. Hand-in-hand with that, identity theft is at an all-time high, with over 1.3 million reports to the Federal Trade Commission (FTC) in 2020. A digital identity would provide Americans with a way to prove who they are online in a more secure manner. People could use it to sign up for government benefits, make a withdrawal from their bank, or to view their medical records, all with the risk of identity theft or fraud approaching zero. Reducing identity fraud would not only provide tremendous savings to individuals and consumers, but would also create massive savings for our government as well.

However, it is important to get this right. We must ensure that a digital identity framework is established with the utmost emphasis on privacy and security. That is why I have introduced the Improving Digital Identity Act of 2021, a bipartisan measure to establish a government-wide approach to improving digital identity. This bill would establish a task force in the Executive Office of the President to develop secure methods for Federal, State, and local agencies to validate identity attributes, to protect the privacy and security of individuals, and to support reliable, interoperable digital identity verification in both the public and private sectors.

This is the first step to determine what our government needs in order to implement this crucial technology. Using the power of AI, we can detect suspicious activity, catch bad actors, and greatly improve our online validation and authentication process.

I thank all of our Members and witnesses for being here today. And I look forward to this discussion to find out how we can best use artificial intelligence and digital identity to improve the lives of everyday Americans.

The Chair now recognizes the ranking member of the task force, Mr. Gonzalez of Ohio, for 5 minutes for an opening statement.

Mr. GONZALEZ OF OHIO. First off, thank you, Chairman Foster, for your leadership on this task force and for today's hearing and the witnesses. I want to commend all of your hard work on this issue, and for being a thoughtful leader in Congress on how to better protect the personally identifiable information (PII) of Americans across the country. I have enjoyed our dialogues on that, and I look forward to continuing them.

Today's hearing provides an opportunity to hear directly from industry experts and stakeholders on advancements in improving the protection of Americans' personal identity. The task force had a similar hearing in 2019, and it is important that we continue to consider gaps that persist, and the proper role for the Federal Government, going forward.

As a consumer, it often feels like you need to share every important detail of your personal identity in order to even think about creating an account with a financial institution or other internet service provider. Sharing your driver's license, Social Security number, sometimes your passport, and other sensitive information online can be intimidating and can make consumers question whether their information is safe and secure.

And it is not hard to see why. Financial services firms fall victim to cybersecurity attacks approximately 300 times more frequently than other businesses. These breaches have occurred as bad actors have become even more sophisticated, and have amassed troves of data on American citizens. This, along with the wealth of data that Americans share daily via social media, has empowered criminals to take advantage of the current identity system which they then use to commit theft and fraud.

To the credit of private industry, we have seen tremendous advances in technology to help secure Americans' private information and identity. The use of AI, machine learning, and blockchain technology has allowed for new forms of analysis that can verify an individual's identity in a secure way.

Now, it is time for Congress to work with Federal regulators to ensure that the United States is equipped with the tools necessary to keep pace internationally. We should consider innovative proposals such as Mr. Foster's Improving Digital Identity Act, which will establish a task force within the Federal Government to engage with relevant stakeholders, but would also require the National Institute of Standards & Technology (NIST) to develop a framework of standards for the Federal Government to follow when providing services to support digital identity verification. I commend him and my other colleagues for their work on this thoughtful legislation.

Beyond the obvious concerns regarding fraud and identity theft, I am also looking forward to learning more today about how other forms of identification verification can increase access to financial services and inclusion. This committee should champion new technologies and their ability to break down the barriers that prevent low-income Americans from accessing critical banking services. Digital identity technologies provide a lot of promise and an opportunity to further inclusion in our financial services space.

I look forward to the discussion today, and I yield back.

Chairman FOSTER. Thank you.

Now, we welcome the testimony of our distinguished witnesses: Jeremy Grant, coordinator of The Better Identity Coalition; David Kelts, director of product development for GET Group North America; Louise Maynard-Atem, research lead at Women in Identity; Elizabeth Renieris, founding director of the Notre Dame-IBM Technology Ethics Lab at the University of Notre Dame; and Victor Fredung, chief executive officer of Shufti Pro.

Witnesses are reminded that their oral testimony will be limited to 5 minutes. You should be able to see a timer on your screen that will indicate how much time you have left, and a chime will go off at the end of your time. I would ask that you be mindful of the time, and quickly wrap up your testimony when you hear the chime, so that we can be respectful of both the witnesses' and the task force members' time.

And without objection, your written statements will be made a part of the record.

I just want to also take this moment to really compliment you on the very high quality of your written testimony. It is worth reading more than once, because of the deep and important observations that it makes about where digital identity is, and should be going in our country.

Mr. Grant, you are now recognized for 5 minutes to give an oral presentation of your testimony.

Statement of Jeremy Grant, Coordinator, the Better Identity Coalition

Mr. GRANT. Thank you.

Chairman Foster, Ranking Member Gonzalez, and members of the task force, thank you for the opportunity to testify today.

I am here on behalf of The Better Identity Coalition, an organization focused on bringing together leading firms from different sectors to work with policymakers to improve the way Americans establish, protect, and verify their identities when they are online. Our members include recognized leaders from financial services, health, technology, Fintech, payments, and security.

Yesterday marked the 3-year anniversary of the release of our identity policy blueprint, which outlined a set of key initiatives the government should launch to improve identity that are both meaningful in impact and practical to implement. Our 24 members are united by a common recognition that the way we handle identity today in the U.S. is broken, and by a common desire to see both the public and private sectors each take steps to make identity systems work better.

On that note, I am very grateful to the AI Task Force for calling this hearing today, as well as to Chairman Foster for his leadership on this topic. The legislation that he and Congressmen Katko, Langevin, and Loudermilk introduced 2 weeks ago, the Improving Digital Identity Act of 2021, is the single best way for government to begin to address the inadequacies of America's identity infrastructure.

I think that one of the top takeaways for the members of this task force today is that identity is critical infrastructure and needs to be treated as such. The Department of Homeland Security (DHS) said as much in 2019, when it declared identity as one of 55 national critical functions, defined as those services so vital to the U.S. that their disruption, corruption, or dysfunction would have a debilitating effect on security.

But compared to other critical functions, identity has gotten scant investment and attention, and the Improving Digital Identity Act, if approved, will get us started. And I think we are overdue to get started. The enormity of the problems that was magnified several times over the last 18 months, amidst the pandemic, literally made it impossible to engage in most in-person transactions. The pandemic laid bare the inadequacies of our digital identity infrastructure, enabling cybercriminals to steal billions of dollars, and creating major barriers for Americans trying to obtain critical benefits and services.

More than $63 billion was stolen from State unemployment insurance programs by cybercriminals exploiting weak ID verification systems, according to the Labor Department. On the flip side, we have seen hundreds of stories of Americans who have been unable to get the benefits they desperately need because their applications for unemployment had been falsely flagged for fraud when they find themselves unable to successfully navigate the convoluted and complicated processes many States have put in place to verify identity.

Beyond unemployment, the inadequacy of our identity infrastructure remains a major challenge in financial services. Last year, the Financial Crimes Enforcement Network (FinCEN) reported that banks were losing more than $1 billion each month due to identity-related cybercrime. Meanwhile, millions of Americans can't get a bank account because they don't have the foundational identity documents needed to prove who they are. And amidst all of this, ID theft losses soared by 42 percent last year.

So, why are there so many problems here? Well, attackers have caught up with a lot of the first-generation tools we have used to protect and verify and authenticate identity. And while this last year might have driven this point home, the reality is that these tools have been vulnerable for quite some time.

There are a lot of reasons for this, but the most important question is, what should government and industry do about it now? If there is one message that the task force should take away from today's hearing, it is that industry said they can't solve this alone. We are at a juncture where the government will need to step up and play a bigger role to help address critical vulnerabilities in our digital identity fabric, and passing the Improving Digital Identity Act is where we should start.

Why is government action needed here? Well, as one of our members noted, the title of this hearing, "I Am Who I Say I Am," is technically incorrect, since for all purposes, when it comes to identity, you are who the government says you are. At the end of the day, government is the only authoritative issuer of identity in the U.S., but identity systems that the government administers are largely stuck in the paper world, whereas commerce has increasingly moved online.

This idea of an identity gap, a complete absence of credentials built to support digital transactions, is being actively exploited by adversaries to steal identities, money, and sensitive data, and defraud consumers, governments, and businesses alike. And while industry has come up with some decent tools to try to get around this identity gap, the adversaries have caught up with many of them.

Going forward, the government will need to take a more active role in working with industry to deliver next-generation remote-ID proofing solutions. This is not about a national ID. We don't recommend that one be created. We already have a number of nationally-recognized authoritative government identity systems: the driver's license; the passport; the Social Security number. But because of this identity gap, the systems are stuck in the paper world while commerce is moving online.

To fix this, America's paper-based system should be modernized around a privacy-protecting, consumer-centric model that allows consumers to ask an agency that issued a credential to stand behind it in the online world, by validating the information from the credential. It is exactly what the Improving Digital Identity Act would do in a way that sets a high bar for privacy, security, and inclusivity.

Thank you for the opportunity to testify today. Note that I have submitted lengthier testimony for the record, including some recommendations on AI and identity. I look forward to answering your questions.

[The prepared statement of Mr. Grant can be found on page 45 of the appendix.]

* * *

Chairman FOSTER. Thank you, Mr. Grant.

Mr. Kelts, you are now recognized for 5 minutes to give an oral presentation of your testimony.

Statement of David Kelts, Director of Product Development, Get Group North America

Mr. KELTS. Thank you, Chairman Foster, Ranking Member Gonzalez, and members of the task force. I appreciate the opportunity today.

I am David Kelts of Arlington, Massachusetts, representing myself in support of mobile driver's licenses and forming governance for an identity ecosystem that reinforces American values of privacy, equity, and freedom, while spurring innovation.

I am the director for product development for GET Group North America, which is piloting the Utah mobile driver's license currently, and I have been a member for over 5 years of the ISO standards working group that wrote the

ISO 18013-5 mobile driver's license standard. I lead the Evangelism Task Force for that group, and I was the lead author on privacy assessment with many international collaborators.

A mobile driver's license (mDL) is a digitally-signed ID document placed on the mobile phone of the correct individual for them to control. Government issuers around the globe are the signers of the identity information, and this signature allows for using an mDL when government-issued ID information is legally required, including for in-person transactions.

You don't show your mDL to someone else. Imagine if we were showing credit card numbers to merchants from our phones. Screenshots and editing tools would result in fraud. Instead, you tap or scan and share a token with the verifier or a reader, and that token can be used to request a subset of the mDL data. The mDL holder has full consent over what they share, and with this standard, people can use the mobile driver's license around the country, and around the globe. So, this minimizing of data to that which is necessary for the transaction represents an improvement over physical cards, where the full data is always printed on the front and found in the barcode on the back.

The ISO 18013-5 mDLs are for fronted data transfer for in-person usage. They are designed, the standard is designed to fit next to other identity standards like OpenID Connect, and things like user authentication from the FIDO Alliance.

There are challenges to empowering Americans with this mobile ID document in order for us to meet the values and goals of all of the people—protecting identity information, giving greater control and flexibility to the rightful holder of the identity, supporting accuracy of these operations—and these come with the goals of improved privacy and inclusivity and access for all. These goals for mDL in person are the same as the goals for identity in cyberspace.

mDL itself sort of naturally forms an ecosystem. The government issuers are the signers of the data, so they have a passive role in lending trust to the transaction. This is in the form of a public key used to validate the accuracy, integrity, and provenance of the data. The technology works today, and is functional, but government issuers must make the first move. This sets challenges in funding a digital transformation that benefits the residents and businesses within anya State. Doing the civic good is not always enough rationale.

Consumer Pays models seem to be taking hold similar to our ID cards but they can require legislative approval and support for this digital transformation at the State level and can keep privacy and American values at the forefront, and kick-start contactless ID.

Market forces alone will not shape an identity-equal system that meets our values and goals. Price pressure on software towards free has been driven by these privacy-invasive data-gathering advertising policies. If the software is free, then you are the product. And kick-starting market forces, if they don't happen, it is possible that entities with very deep pockets can swoop in, meet the market needs, and own an identity ecosystem.

Challenges exist on the business side as well as on the verifier side. Businesses and government agencies will wait for a large number of mDL holders before investing and accepting these digital ID documents. That can leave people with no place to use their digital ID.

Across the globe, there are government-led trust frameworks like Australia, privately-led frameworks like Sovrin, and public-private partnerships like the Pan-Canadian Trust Framework in Canada, launched by the Digital ID & Authentication Council of Canada (DIACC).

I recommend initiating a public-private partnership to define a framework that meets our values and goals from the existing pieces, and that can enforce those requirements. This can kick-start identity solutions of many types to meet our goals in the digital transformation. Federal agencies can continue to lead and lend their expertise to this, and can be incentivized to accept mobile driver's licenses for things like TSA agents to protect their health.

DHS innovation programs can be refocused from architectural goals to deployment of contactless ID technology. And we welcome the continued and expanded participation of the Federal Government and Federal agencies.

Thank you.

[The prepared statement of Mr. Kelts can be found on page 67 of the appendix.]

Chairman FOSTER. Dr. Maynard-Atem, you are now recognized for 5 minutes to give an oral presentation of your testimony.

Statement of Louise Maynard-Atem, Research Lead, Women in Identity

Ms. MAYNARD-ATEM. Good afternoon, and thank you, Chairman Foster, Ranking Member Gonzalez, and members of the task force for the opportunity to testify today.

My name is Louise Maynard-Atem. I am the research lead for the nonprofit organization, Women in Identity. We are an organization whose mission is to ensure that digital identity solutions are designed and built for the diverse communities that they are intended to serve in mind. We are a volunteer-led organization, and we all work full-time in the digital identity sector. We are entirely independent, and not acting in the interests of any one organization or individual, but we are all united by the belief that we need identity systems that work for everyone by ensuring that they are inclusive and free from bias, and that is the specific topic I would like to talk about today.

The need for improved digital identity systems and infrastructure has been a pressing requirement for many years as more businesses have moved their operations online. The pandemic has accelerated that transition, and the need has become more critical in the last 18 months.

The shift presents us with a unique opportunity to enable economic and societal value creation as digital identity systems become the gatekeeper to services like online banking, e-commerce, and insurance. However, we also need to recognize that the use of technology in these systems has the potential to further entrench and potentially exacerbate the exclusionary and bias practices that persist in society today.

Simply digitizing what were previously analogue processes and utilizing flawed data would be a missed opportunity to deliver systems and services that benefit all citizens.

At Women in Identity, we believe inclusion doesn't just happen on its own. For identity systems to be inclusive and free from bias, the requirement must be explicitly mandated. There are countless examples of where exclusion and bias haven't been explicitly mandated against, and in many of those instances, systems have been built that exclude certain groups, often based on characteristics like race, gender, culture, socioeconomic background, or disability.

According to recent population stats in the United States, approximately 11 percent of adults don't have government-issued ID documents, approximately 18 percent of adults don't use a smartphone, and 5.4 percent of U.S. households are unbanked.

Government-issued IDs, ownership of smartphones, and having a bank account can often be the building blocks used for creating digital identity services for individuals. It is essential that any solution that we develop has to be accessible for all of the groups that I have mentioned, and doesn't cause them to be further excluded from opportunities that such technology might present.

If you think about the physical world, we would never erect buildings that weren't accessible to all. Features like wheelchair ramps are mandated. We need to make sure that we are mandating the equivalent accessibility in the digital world.

Within Women in Identity, we have seen a move towards identity trust frameworks being developed, where the need for inclusion and testing for bias is being explicitly called out.

Here in the UK, I wanted to mention the UK digital identity and attributes trust framework that Women in Identity was involved in consulting on. This framework sets out the requirements to help organizations understand what a good identity verification looks like. There are explicit callouts that make sure products and services are exclusive and acceptable, and organizations are required to complete an annual exclusion report to transparently explain if certain users or user groups are excluded and why.

The Information Commissioner in the UK has responded in support of the trust framework, but raises caution if digital identity and attributes systems are relying on automated processing, due to the use of algorithms or artificial intelligence within those systems. Automated decision-making may have discriminatory effects due to bias present in the system design, the algorithms used, or the data sets used in the creation of the product or service.

At Women in Identity, we are currently carrying out a piece of research that seeks to understand the societal and economic impact of exclusion in the context of digital identity, and specifically within financial services.

We hope this research will inform the creation of a code of conduct designed to help solution providers identify and mitigate potential areas of bias and inclusion in product design to ensure that the industry is building products that work for everybody, not just the select few.

To conclude, we believe that in order to achieve the full potential of digital identity systems, inclusion requirements must be specifically and explicitly mandated for within any regulation or legislation, and also, that they must be measured on an ongoing basis. There are a number of examples within my written testimony where I describe how this is being done elsewhere, and I strongly believe in the benefit of sharing best practices and lessons learned with other industry bodies and consumer advocacy groups to ensure that we are delivering systems that enable all citizens equally.

Thank you very much for your time, and I look forward to your questions.

[The prepared statement of Dr. Maynard-Atem can be found on page 80 of the appendix.]

Chairman FOSTER. Thank you, Dr. Maynard-Atem.

Professor Renieris, you are now recognized for 5 minutes to give an oral presentation of your testimony.

Statement of Elizabeth M. Renieris, Professor of the Practice & Founding Director, Notre Dame–IBM Technology Ethics Lab, University of Notre Dame

Ms. RENIERIS. Thank you, Chairman Foster, Ranking Member Gonzalez, and members of the task force for the opportunity to testify before you.

My name is Elizabeth Renieris. I am a professor of the practice and founding director of the Notre Dame-IBM Technology Ethics Lab at the University of Notre Dame, a technology and human rights fellow at the Harvard Kennedy School, and a fellow at Stanford's Digital Civil Society Lab. My research is focused on cross-border data governance frameworks and the ethical and human rights implications of digital identity systems, artificial intelligence, and blockchain and distributed ledger technologies.

I am testifying in my personal capacity, and my views do not necessarily reflect those of any organizations with which I am affiliated.

I began my legal career as an attorney, working on cybersecurity policy at the Department of Homeland Security, and went on to practice as a data protection and privacy lawyer on 3 continents. As a consultant, I have had the opportunity to advise the World Bank, the UK Parliament, the European Commission, and others on data protection, blockchain, AI, and digital identity, and I am grateful for the opportunity to participate in this hearing on this important topic today.

As laid bare by the COVID-19 pandemic, we increasingly depend on digital tools and services for work, school, healthcare, banking, government services, and nearly all aspects of our lives. And unlike when we interact or transact in person, we have limited visibility into who or what is on the other end of a digital interaction or transaction.

Even before the pandemic, vulnerabilities in digital identity systems contributed to a tax on our energy supply, hospitals, financial institutions, and other critical infrastructure. As these sectors are digitized, automated, and algorithmically and computationally manipulated, they increasingly depend on a secure digital identity. As we evolve into a world with the internet in everything, with all manner of internet of things (IoT) devices, sensors, network technologies, and other connected systems, the digital is becoming the built environment. Without secure, reliable, and trustworthy digital identity for people, entities, and things, this new cyber-physical reality is increasingly vulnerable to attacks, threatening individual safety and national security.

Digital identity is becoming critical infrastructure. As dominant technology companies pursue new revenue streams of healthcare, education, financial services, and more, privately owned and operated ID systems with profit-maximizing business models may threaten the privacy, security, and other fundamental rights of individuals and communities. Often, they also incorporate new and advanced technologies such as AI, machine learning, blockchain, and advanced biometrics that are not well-understood and not subject to sufficiently clear legal or governance frameworks.

In order to engender trust, safety, and security with digital ecosystems, we need trustworthy, safe, and security digital identity. And in order to engender trust, safety, and security in our society, we need to deploy it ethically and responsibly.

Recognizing the growing importance of digital identity as critical infrastructure, and seeking to reign in the private control over it, governments in the European Union, Canada, New Zealand, and elsewhere are prioritizing efforts to design and build the infrastructure needed to support robust digital identity.

For example, the European Commission is working on a universally-accepted public electronic identity, or eID, including as an alternative to privacy-invasive solutions such as log-in with Facebook or Google. Even as we have hundreds of frameworks for ethical AI, we lack any specific to digital identity. To remain competitive globally, avoid enclosure of the public sphere through privatized identity schemes, and protect the civil and human rights of Americans, the Federal Government must take the lead in shaping the technical, commercial, legal, and ethical standards for the design, development, and deployment of these systems as critical infrastructure. And the Improving Digital Identity Act is a good first step in that direction.

Such standards must not only include best practices with respect to the privacy and security of data, but also measures for fairness, transparency, and accountability on the part of entities designing and deploying the technology, strong enforcement and oversight, and adequate remedies of redress for the people impacted.

They must also address power asymmetries, the risks of exclusion and discrimination, and the specific challenges associated with the use of blockchain, AI, and other emerging technologies. We must avoid building digital ID systems and infrastructure in a way that would further expand and entrench the surveillance state, as do the national identity systems in India or China.

When we move through the physical world today, we are rarely asked to identify ourselves. But as everything increasingly has a digital component, and as the market for digital ID grows, we are at risk of flipping that paradigm. To avoid the erosion of privacy through persistent and ubiquitous identification, we will also need guardrails around the use of these systems, including when and why identity can be required. If we are not careful, we might go from identity as the exception to identity as the rule.

To summarize my recommendations for Congress, we must recognize that digital identity is critical infrastructure. The Federal Government must lead to create standards for safe, secure, and trustworthy ID. Those standards must address specific challenges associated with new and emerging technologies and ensure public option. And, finally, we need guardrails around the use of ID to avoid ID becoming an enabler of surveillance and control.

Thank you again for the opportunity. I look forward to your questions.

[The prepared statement of Professor Renieris can be found on page 85 of the appendix,]

Chairman FOSTER. Thank you, Professor. And your timing was accurate to the second. So, my compliments on that as well.

Mr. Fredung, you are now recognized for 5 minutes to give an oral presentation of your testimony.

Statement of Victor Fredung, Chief Executive Officer, Shufti Pro

Mr. FREDUNG. Thank you, Chairman Foster, Ranking Member Gonzalez, and distinguished members of the task force. I am excited to be here, and thank you for inviting me to testify before you today on this very important topic.

My name is Victor Fredung, and I am the cofounder and CEO of Shufti Pro. Shufti Pro is an identification and compliance platform that provides services to government agencies and companies throughout the world.

Our service is primarily focused on identification, or what is more commonly referred to as Know Your Customer (KYC), and relies on using automated technology such as artificial intelligence and machine learning, and has successfully been used by companies from all corners of the world to not only verify customers' ID documents, but also verify that the customer is truly who they say they are.

When it comes to identification, most clients utilize our services that combine document verification, face verification, liner check, and optical character recognition, to give accuracy above 99 percent, and to give businesses the assurance that they are taking the appropriate steps to verify their customers.

In addition, we offer what we refer to as a configurable approach to verification flow, and by, "configurable," we mean that we allow the clients to fill out their own verification services and decide on a setting as to how a particular verification should be performed. This is crucial for businesses to comply with different regulatory requirements and configurations that look different throughout the world.

I think we can all agree that the timing of this particular subject is entirely in line. During the pandemic, we witnessed the world turning towards digitalization and relying more and more on the use of the internet for everyday tasks. The problem, however, was that all were not equally competitive.

I would like to discuss a couple of topics with you today, the first involving how AI can help enhance verification of customers. To give you background, we started our journey back in 2017, when most businesses relied on using either a hybrid or a manual approach to verifying customers. A hybrid approach includes, for the most part, a physical person taking a look at an ID document and a selfie to verify if it was the person or not.

The problem with this approach is that, first, it is not scalable. Second, it is also very time-consuming, and then costly for the client using the service. So what we did was begin by using artificial intelligence and machine learning to help protect security interests that can be found on different ID documents, for example, microprinting, sonograms, or even the placement of the text.

We also saw that some customers might try to tamper with portions of the document, perhaps changing their date of birth or their nationality. So, we developed our anti-spoofing technology that also combines text detection, hologram verification, and line effect to accurately verify the customer is who they say they are and that they aren't trying to fake their identity. And by experimenting with the usage of automated technology, we not only saw that verifications could be processed at a much faster pace, we also saw that capturing the identity increased significantly since sophisticated forces can change security features that would bypass you and I.

The second topic I would like to address today is in regard to data privacy and how end users can feel secure when providing their identity. As we all know, data breaches happen to some of the world's biggest companies, and it is usually not the business that suffers the most, it is the end users who get their identities compromised. There are, however, different ways to try and solve this, for example, by utilizing on-device verifications when not only the data is transmitted elsewhere. Another example would be that the providers for the clients do not store any sensitive data involved with the customers. They simply have a specific confirmation that the customer was successfully verified by the appropriate standards and, after that, all of the data is erased. Here it is unfortunately usually a problem, since most frameworks require the data to be kept for X amount of years.

There are also ongoing discussions and experiments as to how to name the blockchain as part of the data sharing, as well as the storage of the customers' data, and how to allow customers to reuse already-proven identities. This is, however, in prototype status at the moment, but it's definitely something to develop in the future.

The last topic I would like to mention is our research into the many different kinds of identity frameworks and the documents that can be combined from across the world. Using the United States as an example, we see different requirements and obligations from different sectors, in addition to each State having its own unique set of ID documents. They do not yet follow the universal framework when it comes to the security features on the documents. This issue presents a problem for a lot of companies, not only in the United States, but all over the world, where requirements, documents, and settings differentiate and no universal framework is applicable.

We strongly applaud the REAL ID Act and the minimum security standards it establishes, and will strongly suggest continued pursuit of a universal framework that each State needs to follow when it comes to the selection of ID documents, and the unified requirement when it comes to what information needs to be verified and how verification should be performed in those States.

I also support Chairman Foster's and Congressman Loudermilk's Improving Digital Identity Act and its purpose of modernizing the ID infrastructure.

Thank you for inviting me to testify today, and I look forward to your questions.

[The prepared statement of Mr. Fredung can be found on page 36 of the appendix.]

Chairman FOSTER. Thank you.

And I will now recognize myself for 5 minutes for questions.

Just to give an initial idea of what scope of improvement we might be able to see if we have widespread use of high-quality mobile ID, if you look at the large, high-profile hacks that have happened, that have hit the headlines, the Colonial Pipeline, the DCCC hack of a few years back, what fraction of these would be largely eliminated if we had widespread use of a mobile ID second-factor authentication instead of just passwords?

Mr. GRANT. I am happy to jump in, if I can.

I think it is an anomaly these days when a major incident happens and identity is not the attack vector, although I want to just differentiate—when we talk identity, to me, we are talking about two things: identity proofing, what you are doing when you are opening an account; and authentication, how you log in after you have already opened an account.

I think a lot of the fraud we have seen in unemployment systems has been taking advantage of the identity proofing challenge. How do you prove you are really Bill Foster for the first time, and which Bill Foster, given that there are probably several thousand of you? There, we basically saw stolen data used to cut through whatever protections a lot of States had in place, or in some cases, they had none at all, to steal billions of dollars.

With regard to some of the other breaches that we have seen, Colonial Pipeline, some things with ransomware, there it is much more focused on authentication, how you compromise a password, or even, in some cases, compromise some first-generation forms of multifactor authentication, like ones that are based on a code that is texted to you that is now phishable as well.

I think, overall, with both identity proofing and authentication, we have big problems. If we could close both of those gaps, you really start to raise the cost of the tax for a lot of criminals and make it much harder for them to do the things that they have been doing.

Chairman FOSTER. Okay. One of the things that I think many of you have mentioned in your testimony was how COVID has sort of changed the profile of identity and the need, the fact that we are moving more and more online. It is becoming more important.

The other thing that has happened is that there is real bipartisan agreement that we have to get a broadband connection to essentially all Americans, and that there is a real Federal role in subsidizing that. I think that at last count, the Republican talking number was $65 billion that should be dedicated to this. The Democrat counteroffer was $100 billion. But if we end up anywhere in between those two numbers, we are going to have a real step forward in closing the digital divide and getting at least a low-end digital device in the hands of all Americans and a broadband account.

And so, given that, how would you then piggyback products, for example, digital driver's licenses or other ways? How do we get this, so that it is the second part of provisioning a broadband and digital identity to people? Anyone who wishes to answer that.

Mr. KELTS. Yes, I think that access to broadband, that access to connectivity and phones will help to increase accessibility to everyone, and I would say, to the same level of accessibility as getting an ID card that you currently have, and being able to use that.

The technology in mDL, I will speak specifically about that, is geared to use on really any phone, because there are multiple ways that you can interact with that for in-person, and we expect we can cover the vast majority of phones that are out there, provided they have either a screen or NFC or something that allows for the transmission. So, I think that would be a huge step towards accessibility for everyone on mobile identities.

Chairman FOSTER. And when we do this, how do we make sure that the equity issues are addressed properly? Why don't we let the Ph.D. material scientists weigh in on this. They seem to be very interested and involved in this set of issues.

Ms. MAYNARD-ATEM. I think as soon as you start to drive access for everybody, then there are lots of solutions you can put in place. If we are establishing a baseline of, everyone has access to some kind of device, then I think that really levels the playing field. It is not saying, everyone needs to have a smartphone. It is just saying, everyone needs to have access to something. I think that is a big hurdle.

Certainly in the UK, we are going at it from a vouching standpoint. So if you don't have access, you can say someone says, "you are you," and we can take that as standard. But if there is an ability to provide everybody with some kind of technology so that they can use these services, then I think that really moves the accessibility debate really far forward.

Chairman FOSTER. And you mentioned, I think, in your testimony, the eID effort in the EU. Is that correct?

Oops, I am out of time here. Okay.

Let's see. For Members who are interested, if there is time, we are probably going to be able to have time for a second round. And if that fails, we will continue our tradition of, at the end of the formal part of the hearing, I will gavel it closed, and we can just sit around and talk, sort of the Zoom equivalent of just hanging around in the anteroom and talking with our witnesses, which is often the most valuable part of a hearing.

I will now recognize the ranking member of the task force, Mr. Gonzalez of Ohio, for 5 minutes.

Mr. GONZALEZ OF OHIO. Thank you, Mr. Chairman, for holding this hearing and for our great witnesses here today.

Before I get started, I ask for unanimous consent to add to the record a letter from the National Association of Convenience Stores, please.

Chairman FOSTER. Without objection, it is so ordered.

Mr. GONZALEZ OF OHIO. Thank you.

Mr. Grant, I want to start with you. It is good to see you, and I look forward to reconnecting down the road.

As we were talking yesterday a bit offline, I told you I am excited to support Chairman Foster's Improving Digital Identity Act. I think it is a step in the right direction for sure.

My question is, beyond the Improving Digital Identity Act, what additional areas should this committee be focused on from a legislative standpoint, with respect to digital ID?

Mr. GRANT. Thank you for the question, Congressman. It's good to see you again.

I would say the Foster bill is a great place to start in that it finally starts to pull together what I would call a whole-of-government approach to looking at this issue. And one of the challenges I think we have in the U.S. is that we have nationally-recognized authoritative identity systems, but they are split between the Federal, State, and local levels. I got my birth certificate from the county I was born in. The State DMV gives me my driver's license. And I have a passport from the U.S. State Department.

And what is great about that bill is it starts to take a look at, how do you take a consistent standards-based approach so that any American could ask any of those entities to vouch for them when they are trying to prove who they are online? And as I mentioned in my opening statement, NIST also has set a high bar for security and privacy.

I think the big question that is going to come beyond that is going to be how to fund some of that, particularly in the States where—I know that David Kelts talked a little about the work he is doing with mobile driver's licenses. I think there is a concern that while there is a handful of States doing things there now, if we are not going to actually invest dollars in trying to jump-start that activity in the States, that it might be, say, 15 years before we start to get to critical mass of people having some digital corollary to their paper documents, and that is going to be a real issue. And I think the infrastructure bill that is being negotiated, as Chairman Foster pointed out, could be a great place to put some money in to help accelerate that.

I think beyond that, the more AI is going to be used, there are probably going to be more questions to be asked. And this task force is obviously going to be a great place to evaluate some of those considerations.

Mr. GONZALEZ OF OHIO. Great.

Ms. Renieris, same question for you. I am not sure if you are familiar with the legislation, but just areas beyond that it we should be considering at the committee level to foster greater adoption of digital ID.

Ms. RENIERIS. Sure. Thank you for the question.

I would say first on the legislation in particular, I would just like to point out one red flag that I am concerned about, which is a reliance on consumer consent. As we have been having conversations around State and Federal privacy legislation, I think there is growing awareness around some of the limitations on consent-based frameworks in this context. So, in going forward, it might be worth reconsidering sort of the basis for some of the personal data processing involved in these identity systems.

Separate and apart from that, really I think a lot of this is the question of the underlying infrastructure in other sectors. For example, even if you had a really robust whole-of-government approach, and created sufficient privacy and security technical standards through NIST or otherwise, you would still have a problem, for example, if our healthcare infrastructure can't ingest those standards or those technologies.

So, we really have to think about other upgrades across the infrastructure in other sectors in order for digital ID to be woven in and layered on top.

And I think the third thing is really something that has already been pointed out around mandating inclusion in the conversation. I think, as we have expressed in our testimonies, and as we have seen in the field, there can be a real lack of diversity in these conversations. And so in addition to the interagency kind of diversity, I think the diversity of expertise and voices at the table is really critical.

Mr. GONZALEZ OF OHIO. Thank you.

And then, Mr. Kelts, with the pilot program in Utah, what are you learning? And I am looking for sort of barriers, things that have been difficult, that this committee should have on our minds as that program has unfolded.

Mr. KELTS. I think that the demands we have seen from consumers has been larger than expected, which has been great. We are very early in the pilot program and positioning people. That is a key thing. And as well, the demand from business, the ability for the State Government to engage businesses along the whole process right from the beginning of the RFP process, and to engage those stakeholders has been a huge advantage for making this work in Utah.

Mr. GONZALEZ OF OHIO. Good. I see I am out of time.

I yield back, Mr. Chairman.

Chairman FOSTER. Thank you.

The Chair will now recognize the Chair of the full Financial Services Committee, the gentlewoman from California, Chairwoman Waters, for 5 minutes of questions.

Chairwoman WATERS. Thank you very much. I am on now.

First of all, Mr. Foster, I want to thank you for the attention that you have paid to this identification issue, and the work that you are doing that is so important.

I would like to ask Dr. Maynard-Atem a question, and if this has been answered already, then I won't proceed with it and I can talk about it with you later on. It is about the use of artificial intelligence, of course, for individual identification that has raised concerns about algorithms of bias.

As you know, smartphone authentication can employ voice or facial recognition technologies, but these technologies have been shown to exhibit bias against women and minorities. In fact, researchers have found that facial recognition technologies falsely identified Black and Asian faces 10 to 100 times more than White ones, and falsely identified women more than they did men.

Do you have any concerns that a digital identity system could also exhibit this kind of bias? If so, what steps need to be taken to eliminate this bias?

Ms. MAYNARD-ATEM. Absolutely. Thank you for that question.

I think there is always the risk that if you are starting to introduce emerging technologies, emerged technologies like artificial intelligence and machine learning, you run the risk of bias creeping in, depending on the way that those systems have been built, and the data those systems have been tested upon. I think a lot of the issues arise from very homogenous test data being used to actually test these systems. So, when they are learning how to recognize faces, they are tested and trained on a very homogeneous data set which might be all male, it might be majority-male, or it might be a majority of people of one particular race.

And I think the way that we sort of overcorrect for that is by ensuring that the data that we are using to build algorithms, to build these things that detect facial characteristics of men and women and races of all colors, to make sure that test data is as diverse as the population that the system is going to serve. We need to make sure that we are equally representing all genders and all races in all of that test data, so the algorithms actually learn to recognize everybody equally rather than situations we have had previously, where they have led specifically to recognize one person or one type of person at the detriment potentially of others.

Chairwoman WATERS. What you are describing is precisely what was discovered a long time ago with medicine and the lack of diversity in the testing that has not led to the ability to deal with some of the problems that we have found in minority communities, Black communities in particular. And so, you do think that this is an important part of moving forward with any identification, absolutely having the kind of diversity and the testing that will bring us the results that we need.

I don't know if this is a good question or not, but I think we have improved the testing in medicine, and particularly with certain diseases where they had to work hard to get minorities in the testing programs. But do you know whether or not it is proven that this has really taken place with medicine, and that the corrections have been made, and they have been able to advance the pharmaceutical products based on the testing that was done, because they know what is needed in a particular minority group? Do you know anything about that?

Ms. MAYNARD-ATEM. I don't know specifically whether or not it has been proven that it has been done, but I think the key point here is that, like I said in my testimony, these things, inclusion, calling out bias, don't just happen on their own, and I think that they need to be mandated. I think we need to call out specifically in legislation that you have to test for these things. You have to test for bias, and you have to make sure that people are included, and you have to test that on an ongoing basis. This can't just be something that you do once and then put it on the shelf and never address again. You have to test. In the UK, it is proposed that it is being done on an annual basis for digital identity systems. We need to be testing and retesting to ensure that any bias that does exist in systems is called out, is explained, and then action plans are put in place to make sure that exclusionary technique or system doesn't then persist going forward.

Chairwoman WATERS. Thank you very much. I appreciate that information. And I will follow up with my colleague, Mr. Foster, and you, as we move forward with this whole issue. Thank you.

I yield back the balance of my time.

Chairman FOSTER. Thank you.

The Chair will now recognize our colleague from North Carolina, Mr. Budd, for 5 minutes.

Mr. BUDD. I thank the Chair, and I also want to thank the witnesses for being here today. It is a very insightful hearing.

Mr. Fredung, I want to direct my questions to you this morning in the brief time we have. With the continued growth in the expanding use of cryptocurrencies, we have seen an increased rollout by exchanges becoming compliant with anti-money laundering. How are these Know Your Customer programs performing compared to traditional finance counterparts?

Mr. FREDUNG. First of all, thank you, Congressman, for that question.

As we all know, cryptocurrency is getting more and more use in the world, not only for investment opportunities but also for everyday tasks. When it comes to the legislation and capturing the criminals as well, we do see it happening with a few different changes here and there as well. Unfortunately, the problem we have seen in the space at this moment is there is not really too much legislation when it comes to cryptocurrency and changes.

As an example, here in Europe we have the Stony licensing. We also have it in the United Kingdom, which has just started issuing different licenses where, if you selected a client, this is a problem we have seen in the space that there needs to be an easier way for different businesses that operate the cryptocurrency exchange to become licensed, and essentially offering customers to buy cryptocurrencies from them.

I would like to bring up here as well that I do believe Shing (ph) analysis company spoke in one of the previous hearings as well where they also discussed, in other words, to the bad actors of the use in cryptocurrency. And I think they also mentioned it was a number of around 0.4 percent which is a decrease from previous years as well.

But as the world is becoming more adapted towards cryptocurrency, I believe the technology providers are also facilitating the identification and verification of customers, and there are plenty of good tools available to help them protect against illegal crypto transactions, alongside a strict company process. So I would say most businesses pretty much have a good defense at the moment to be able to use the space.

Mr. BUDD. Very good. Thank you for that.

So as technology continues to advance and as we look for new ways to identify consumers without jeopardizing their data, which is key, how could we utilize the blockchain as a tool for digital identity verification?

And that will also be for you.

Mr. FREDUNG. Usually, the blockchain for security purposes is very interesting, and as mentioned, definitely something to look out for in the future, and by enabling the usage of blockchain, it helps a lot of the issues which are key, such as unauthorized access to customer data, which is a secure way of transmitting user data, as well as having a better user experience as well. Yes, I think we can all understand that for a customer to set a goal for verification process over and over again, it is not really a user-seamless experience.

In addition to the data privacy area, there are other approaches using blockchain as well. There could also be essentially using one device verification where normally the data is transmitted elsewhere as well.

Mr. BUDD. Financial institutions are subject to a patchwork of statements, data, security, and breach identification laws here in the U.S., State by State. So, in addition to Federal regulations that we saw in the Gramm-Leach-Bliley Act years ago, there is no Federal standard for data security for nonfinancial institutions that handle consumer data. What regulatory improvements would you suggest?

And that is also for you.

Mr. FREDUNG. When it comes to improvements in the regulatory frameworks, there are a few different selections that I would like to bring forward, the first one being a universal framework and requirements and security standards online.

The second one would be an update to the existing ID documents issued by the States, by modernizing the security features located on documents, making it harder for fraudsters to try and tamper with information.

Maybe, in addition, also requiring a line check to be performed. This is something that we do see, but it is not a requirement in all of the different frameworks that we come across. This is essentially a great tool to defend against the easier troll attempts.

Apart from that, we do heavily conduct research in regard to these matters and we would be delighted to share that with the office that is requesting this as well.

Mr. BUDD. I really appreciate that.

That is all of the questions I have. I appreciate your generosity with your time, and also the whole panel.

I yield back to the Chair.

Chairman FOSTER. Thank you.

And the Chair will now recognize my colleague from Illinois, Mr. Casten, for 5 minutes.

Mr. CASTEN. Thank you so much, and I really want to thank you for holding this hearing. You have been leading on this for a long time, Chairman Foster, and we wouldn't be doing this but for your leadership and, my goodness, it is obvious that we need to be doing this. So thank you.

I want to direct my questions to Ms. Renieris. The first is, over the last couple of years, there has been talk of—I think both Google and Apple have talked about introducing a digital driver's license, a digitization of your driver's license on the mobile apps. Do you have any ethical concerns with, essentially, a private digital ID, supplanting a government-managed digital ID?

Ms. RENIERIS. Thank you very much for the question, Congressman.

This is an issue I alluded to in my testimony, and I go into more depth in my written testimony. What Apple and Google have basically done is created the digital wallet infrastructure to host a digitized version of your government-issued driver's license, or your analogue physical ID at this point. It is quite telling that what they have created is not necessarily a digitally native ID, but, rather, a digital version of those artifacts that we are all used to, and I think that is an important distinction.

It is true that they have very sophisticated capabilities now embedded into smartphones, including improved secure enclaves and other technologies, localized machine learning and data processing, that improve some of the data security and privacy aspects of the mobile digital wallet and the credentials stored therein.

But there are serious ethical, and also privacy concerns I have going beyond the data itself. Specifically, I have concerns around incentives and business models. What we have seen over and over again is that a lot of the business models and sort of commercial incentives around the products and services provided by some of the companies you mentioned, including Apple and Google, are not necessarily business models that support civic interests and the values that we are really concerned about, and they actually very often cut against those.

For example, with the Apple ID, we don't yet know exactly what the business model is. However, it is basically the same technology as Apple Pay, which we know has transaction fees associated with it for different players in the ecosystem. So, you can start to see how, depending on the business model and the commercial incentives, this could create perverse incentives for the use of ID, perhaps in contexts where it is not necessary or it didn't exist before.

I also have concerns about the ease of use. The easier and sleeker these credentials are, it feels like it's not a big deal. We start to normalize things like biometrics. We start to normalize presenting our ID in contexts where perhaps it shouldn't be appropriate or required.

So, I think there are concerns that go beyond the data. When we just think about the security and privacy of data, we lose sight of the security and privacy of people, and those are two very different things and the technology designing and building these systems has a very narrow definition of privacy, which is really a technical mathematical view of it.

We have to sort of resituate identity in the context of this socio-technical system that it is, in the context of culture and law and economics and all of these other things to think about what the true impact will be on people, rather than looking at a specific tool or a specific technology.

Mr. CASTEN. Thank you for that. This is a question that obviously gets beyond digital ID and, of course, spans every committee in Congress, but because we are on the Financial Services Committee, we spend a lot of time and we have crafted a lot of regulations around, what happens if I give my money to someone who is a custodian of that money, and we have developed fiduciary rules of looking out for the best interests of that money, and arguably our data is a link to our money and a lot more, as you point out. There have been some people who have talked about, should we create a fiduciary rule that applies to people who hold our data?

I am curious if you have heard any of those proposals, if you are familiar with them, and if you have any thoughts on that as a possible way through some of this morass. Should the private sector get ahead of us? Because once people turn the data over, you can't put the genie back in the bottle, I don't think. So, your thoughts on a fiduciary rule for data?

Ms. RENIERIS. I think that certain fiduciary duties of confidentiality and loyalties and others associated with entities for processing and restoring data can make sense. I think it is sort of a small piece of a much more comprehensive approach that we need. Obviously, it's an approach that, at the moment, is very disjointed across State and Federal proposals.

I do think that we need to think about what is the underlying and legal infrastructure that we have in terms of privacy and data security and data protection. But, again, those are just sort of one piece of a more comprehensive framework that we need. We may also need to think about identity-specific data-related government frameworks, for example, the culmination of data privacy and digital identity infrastructure and pointing out kind of areas where those frameworks overlap and where they diverge and try to reconcile them. But they are a big piece of this.

Mr. CASTEN. Thank you so much, and I yield back.

Chairman FOSTER. Thank you. And we will now recognize our colleague from Texas, Mr. Taylor, for 5 minutes.

Mr. TAYLOR. Thank you, Mr. Chairman. I appreciate this hearing. I think this is an important topic. Mr. Grant, in your written testimony, you mentioned theft from unemployment programs. I have talked to some of my colleagues who were pretty mortified by the billions and billions of dollars that were stolen because of unfortunate loopholes in the administration of those programs. And I realize that digital ID is a component of fighting against that fraud. How do you see AI working with existing frameworks on a way to combat fraud in unemployment insurance?

Mr. GRANT. I think the way I look at it, there is both a—how would I say it? When I look at solving identity, identity is one part of broader fraud reduction and handling risk there. And I think solving this issue presents a couple of different dimensions where, even outside of the things that you might be doing on identity for verification, you might have AI, running broader fraud prevention systems, to be looking at some different signals.

Now, I will say, my take is probably two-thirds to three quarters of those are going to be identity-related in terms of, are you able to, say, sniff out how somebody is potentially using stolen data, or see something about the device they are logging in on that is exhibiting signs that might be about entering the data rather than an individual? I think a lot of it is going to come to identity at the end of day. But there is certainly, I think, broader places we are seeing a lot of these same companies in this space look at things that touch other elements beyond individual identity.

Mr. TAYLOR. And just to my colleagues, I will be trying to work on getting AI language into some of the appropriations to try and prevent fraud. I think that is something that we should begin to look at and start to think about. And, obviously, being the AI Task Force, it is a germane topically to what we do.

Shifting over, Professor Renieris, just to ask you a question about identity technology gone wrong, and obviously, I think it is really important, what Chairman Foster said at the beginning is that we want to have an identity system which really is consistent with our values as Americans: protecting identity; and protecting information.

I kind of think about China and how the Chinese Communist Party's control of digital payments is able to control people's movements, and to stop people who are not in favor of the Chinese Communist Party from being able to buy a plane ticket, and if they are really not in favor, not even to buy a train ticket, or ride a bus.

And so, I am thinking about the technology, in my mind, being abused to really suppress people in a way that is Orwellian. Can you give us examples of other ways that identity technology has gone wrong, not necessarily in this country, but in other countries?

Ms. RENIERIS. Thank you for the question, Congressman. There are many examples. I think one of the most important things to point out is that in a lot of other countries, the digital identity systems are basically mandated national ID schemes that are tied to civil registration and vital statistics. So, if you can't obtain a digital identity in those countries, you are effectively locked out of life. There is basically nothing you can do, and you don't exist. And so, I think that is the broad-level risk.

The second layer of that is that in a lot of countries, what we have seen with digital ID schemes gone wrong, is they tried to integrate—they basically used a single identifier, for example, the Aadhaar number in India. And that single identifier is able to track your activity across all facets of your life, from employment, to healthcare, school, and pretty much everything you do. So, that is another area where you can't retain sort of autonomy over specific domains of your life, for example, you can't separate your personal and professional reputation. And you can't have this kind of contextualized personal identity. So, I think that is also really problematic. It is also problematic from the standpoint of data security. If it can compromise your number, you have concerns around that.

I think going back to the point about inclusion, a lot of these systems were designed without thinking outside of the technology. So, for example, there are countries where women are disproportionately less connected and don't have access to things like mobile devices. And in those countries where digital identity is now through a mobile device, they are basically at the mercy of a partner or someone else to exist and to operate in that country.

Again, a reason to look beyond mutual privacy and security of data and the specific parameters of the technology and think about how they operate in a national context. I go into more detail in my written testimony.

Mr. TAYLOR. Thank you for that answer.

Mr. Chairman, I yield back.

Chairman FOSTER. Thank you. The Chair now recognizes our colleague from North Carolina, Ms. Adams, for 5 minutes.

Ms. ADAMS. Thank you very much, Chairman Foster, Ranking Member Gonzalez, and also Chairwoman Waters for holding this hearing. And to the witnesses, thank you for your testimony as well.

Bias in AI algorithms is a common and widespread concern as the technology has become more entrenched in our daily lives. And I recall distinctly a few years back, when facial recognition software falsely identified my late Congressional Black Caucus colleague, John Lewis, as a criminal. This very real problem that biased AI is having real-world impacts does deserve our scrutiny. So, I am glad that we are having these discussions.

And that is why I fought successfully to include language in our annual appropriations package that asks the National Science Foundation to partner with NGOs and academic institutions to study algorithmic bias more intently.

Professor Renieris, in your testimony, you noted that mistakes in AI ID verification can have significant consequences. So, how can we stop the digital identity process from becoming overly reliant on potentially-flawed AI algorithms? And what role should the Federal Government and State Governments play in the distribution of digital identity?

Ms. RENIERIS. Thank you for the question, Congresswoman. I think this is one of the most important questions and most important conversations to have around digital identity. Going back to Dr. Maynard-Atem's comments about the quality of data, I think, of course, that is a really important consideration. And I actually do think that we are making progress there. Parties who are designing these systems are more cognizant of the need for the data sets to reflect the populations that these systems will operate in.

However, I think what we are not looking at this closely is who is designing and building these technologies in the first place. Regardless of how good underlying data is, risks are not going to be identified by people if we only have homogeneous teams building these things, because they can only perceive the risk that they have been exposed to or that they understand.

The people building these things need to spot these risks in advance and be able to flag them, mitigate them, and build them into the design of the technology. So, there are certainly concerns around bias in the algorithms, but there are concerns in all of the different components of this that flows throughout.

Earlier, we talked about different kinds of biometrics, like face and voice, which we know are subject to both gender and racial bias. But, increasingly, the future is looking into things like behavioral biometrics, which are essentially profiling technologies. Those are also going to raise concerns about equity discrimination, privacy, and inclusion.

I think again, to make this sustainable and sort of forward-looking, the bad actors are always going to be able to outsmart the sort of state-of-the-art of the technology. So, the only way to get ahead of this is to think about how these technologies operate broadly in these socio-technical systems. But you are absolutely right, that is a primary concern in this space. Thank you so much.

Ms. ADAMS. Mr. Grant, despite some of the problems we have discussed today, there are undoubtedly benefits to employing AI to protect consumers. With the increase in data breaches, particularly at credit reporting agencies where large amounts of personally identifiable information has been exposed, how can the AI help with distinguishing between legitimate and illegitimate histories of activities to detect or prevent digital identity fraud?

Mr. GRANT. Thank you for the question, Congresswoman. Before I answer that, I would love piggyback on what Ms. Renieris said, in that, I think as we are concerned about bias, and I think this plays into your question as well here, so much of what we are dealing with in AI are predictive systems that are essentially trying to use AI and machine learning to guess what at the end of the day, only the government really knows. I believe, and I talked about this in my written testimony, that one of the best things the government can do would be to advance the bill Chairman Foster recently introduced, in that it brings in that deterministic layer, what is actually in authoritative government identity systems to complement the probabilistic layer. And I think that is going to be one way to address concerns about bias.

In terms of how AI is being used more constructively, particularly, when we just have terabytes of stolen identity data that is now being used to commit identity fraud, I think one thing we are seeing is a lot vendors out there when they can actually identify, say, what an organized crime ring is doing. AI can study how they enter data and then be able to analyze that and learn whether it is, what it looks like somebody is doing when they are interacting with the device, how they are holding it. Some of these things do tap into behavioral.

But if you can start to learn what looks like it might be malicious behavior, you can then start to generate alerts that might kick some of those applications in a way that if it doesn't block it, it at least kicks off a secondary layer of examination where you can make a more informed decision.

Ms. ADAMS. Thank you, sir. I am out of time. Mr. Chairman, I yield back.

Chairman FOSTER. Thank you. And we will now recognize our colleague from Massachusetts, Mr. Auchincloss, for 5 minutes.

Mr. AUCHINCLOSS. Chairman Foster, thank you for putting this hearing together, and I want to echo your comments at the beginning of this session complimenting our witnesses for the excellence of their written testimony. I thought it was superb. We certainly learned a lot. So, I appreciate that.

Mr. Grant, in your oral testimony, you talk about improving the Digital Identity Act. What element of that would be asking the National Institute of Standards & Technology to really take the lead on setting the protocols and the standards for identity proofing, which as you said is sort of the harder part, would look like? I want to dig into that a little bit with you.

Could you tell us maybe the three Ws of that: who should be involved in that process with NIST; what a good product might look like; and when we would be looking for that to be accomplished? What kind of timeframe is that going to take?

Mr. GRANT. Sure. I think, just in terms of background, Chairman Foster's bill focuses a lot on this. I think it is a way to try and address a lot of the concerns we have heard about today. In terms of whether it is a public sector or a private sector developing some of these systems, how do you come up with standards and best practices that can actually set a high bar for privacy, for security, for inclusion? I think a lot of concerns that people might have about different industry solutions or even a government solution running amuck and losing sight of the importance of the high bar in all of those areas can be accomplished with standards.

As background for the hearing, I discussed in my written testimony that I used to lead the Trusted Identities Group at NIST several years ago. NIST has a great way to engage with stakeholders, not just nationally, but globally, from across the public and private sectors.

And so, I think a benefit of having NIST lead this is that they can, frankly, bring in, whether it is technical experts, like David and Louise, or academics like Elizabeth, or entrepreneurs like Victor, to all come and provide different inputs and then weigh them and synthesize them in a way that gets some outcomes that I think might address all of those issues.

I think the, "what," is not just technical standards, but it is also the business practices. How do you collect data? What recourse do people have? If something goes wrong, how do you protect it? Really, what do I need to know beyond just following the technical standards?

And the, "when," NIST has tackled this for the cybersecurity framework, the privacy framework. In 12 months, it is an elevated or escalated timeframe. My former NIST colleagues will probably be frowning at me if they are watching this now because it is a lot of work to get done in a year. But this is a national crisis. We can get it done.

Mr. AUCHINCLOSS. Professor Renieris, you mentioned identity as a socio-technical construction, which I think it is great way to frame it. From your perspective, what would you want to be seeing from a NIST product that would give you confidence that we are architecting government identity proofing in a way that is not going to lend itself to abuse, and also to my colleague, Mr. Taylor's, point is not going to lend itself to an inappropriate amount of government-concentrated power?

Ms. RENIERIS. Thank you for the question, Congressman. It is an interesting question with regard to NIST. NIST, of course, is focused on technical standards. I would say the advantage of having NIST lead on this front is that they are not subject to some of the perverse incentives I was talking about earlier, in that they have a very long and comprehensive track record of designing standards in a way with the right incentives and considerations in mind.

That said, I think that it is important within NIST, of course, that other experts are consulted, that there are these different types of expertise that I mentioned that go beyond sort of narrow mathematical, technical, and engineering conceptions of these things, which NIST has done before, and in their identity guidance has also been very mindful of some of those considerations.

Now, proofing is considered a relatively technical exercise. But to Mr. Grant's point, I think the reason it is so important is because it is really the gateway to all of this.

It is a critical first step. And what is really nice about that is if we rely on authoritative government-issued identities, those are already accounting for some of those things that I was talking about, and they are not being designed by a computer scientist exclusively.

They are rooted to real-world socio-technical concepts as it is, so they are sort of a good foundation there. And, again, this is something I go into a bit more detail in my statement.

Mr. AUCHINCLOSS. I am going to jump in for the last 15 seconds for Mr. Grant, just because it is a subject of conversation. Increasingly, two-factor authentication as a way to do identity authentication, basically two orthogonal means of identifying itself with a password and then your text message or a Google app, or whatever, is that still the best standard for identity authentication?

Mr. GRANT. For authentication, yes. There is no such thing as a secure password these days. And, in fact, my old colleagues at NIST have told you the guidance of uppercase and lowercase and symbols and numbers. Even a 64-character password can with get phished.

I think the big challenge these days is that even some two-factor—the attackers have caught up with, they can phish the SMS codes, they can trick you into handing over the one-time pass code. I use the FIDO security key, which is a hardware key that can't be phished. I think that is where things need to move to is authentication using things like the FIDO standards based on public key cryptography.

Mr. AUCHINCLOSS. And I am out of time. So, Mr. Chairman, I will yield back.

Chairman FOSTER. Thank you. And I guess we have Member interest in another round of questions, so I will begin by recognizing myself for another 5 minutes.

As part of the infrastructure package to federally subsidize the deployment of mobile IDs in the different States, it gives us an opportunity to set our own standards for privacy and other important aspects.

What are the redlines for privacy that we should really keep our eye on, and insist have to be present? Ones that get mentioned frequently, for example, are no silent interrogation of your app, that the user should be aware every time the ID is presented.

Another one that has been encountered is at a traffic stop when you are asked to present your digital ID, you do not have to turn over your physical cell phone; you simply have some form of electronic communication so the law enforcement officer doesn't get to paw around your cell phone and see what else might be there.

Is there a good list somewhere? And what should be at the top of that list for insisting on from a privacy point of view?

Mr. KELTS. I think there are very good lists. And in my written testimony, I pulled together a number of them that I think can be used and represent sort of a diverse cross section of what has been looked at so far in privacy.

I would add to the list that you, that you included, Chairman Foster. I would add that one of the most difficult things to try to protect against is a surveillance or tracking or aggregating data and then sifting through that data to find usage patterns.

So I think the ability to use paralyzed identifiers, individual identifiers for each transaction, tokens instead of uniform identifiers, and then being able—like enforcing not having central repositories to report usage, I think that is one of the tougher problems, but absolutely key to enforcing privacy for people who are going to use their digital identity and their trust in that.

Chairman FOSTER. Yes. Do any other witnesses have something to add to that?

Mr. GRANT. I would just flag, I think, what is important really is to have a process that looks at privacy risk holistically. And one of the things when I was at NIST that we launched out of the interstate program at the time was the Privacy Engineering Program, which was focused on, how do you look at sort of a soup to nuts approach of privacy from different contexts and identify risks in any system, and then come up with technical or policy mitigations to architect around them? That led to the NIST Privacy Framework. That was something, actually, that the previous Administration had asked NIST to do.

I think one reason I am excited that your legislation would have NIST focused here is it is the one place, frankly, in government or industry that I have seen that has a comprehensive framework that is specifically geared toward identity and security systems.

Beyond that, I think the ability to granularly release certain data about yourself without others—when I look at how many copies of my driver's license might be online, especially over the last year, it is not really important for a lot of those entities to know everything about me. They might just need to know that I am over 21 if I was ordering whiskey during the pandemic, which I might have done once or twice, or that I am eligible for something else. I think being able to focus just on sharing specific things about myself without all of my data, is going to be quite important.

Ms. RENIERIS. If I could also jump in, I think one of the important things to recognize is the need to go upstream. By the time the data is collected or captured, it is often too late to have effective privacy protections in place. So, we really do need to think about data minimization and other techniques. Certainly, privacy-enhancing technology is playing an important role here.

But a concern there, of course, is that they often are very complex, which can result in a lot of user error. So, we also have to think about things like design. We are really moving away from the graphical user interface. We have other types of interfaces that we are moving into in the future. So, we are not going to be able to present long and cumbersome privacy notices and expect people to be able to ingest them and really understand what is happening.

So, design is growing more critically in importance there. Particularly, the faster and sleeker these credentials can be used and the quicker the interaction is, the more important that the design, sort of on the back end and the front end, and also in terms of the privacy standards and engineering, is really front and center before we talk about what we do with the data.

Chairman FOSTER. Thank you. And one of the killer apps for this, as it were, is Central Bank Digital Currencies (CBDCs), which the Financial Services Committee is very involved in. And that immediately gets into international usage, because digital dollars should be useful for people around the world, and we are going to have to authenticate participants. What is the status of international interoperability of these various ID initiatives?

Mr. GRANT. Well, I would say at least from a regulatory perspective in the banking world, it was about a year-and-a half-ago that the Financial Action Task Force (FATF), which is the body of global financial regulators that work together, put out digital identity guidelines. But I would say it is much more of a cookbook in terms of how each country should look to design digital identity systems for some of these types of applications, including potentially CBDCs.

In terms of true interoperability, I think a lot of it is going to have to focus on different countries, including the U.S. developing digital identity infrastructure, and then finding ways, whether it is through treaty negotiations or other mechanisms, to mutually recognize them, and I don't think we are there yet.

Chairman FOSTER. Thank you. And I now recognize Ranking Member Gonzalez for 5 minutes.

Mr. GONZALEZ OF OHIO. Thank you, Mr. Chairman. I am going to probably just stay on one track around Know Your Customer (KYC) and Anti-Money Laundering (AML). And this is for Mr. Grant. It is widely reported that the basics of traditional identity information that the government requires thanks to user KYC, AML, so, name, address, Social Security number, et cetera, are widely for sale on the dark web. I, too, may have purchased some things online to get me through the pandemic. And you just never quite know where all that information ends up. But it doesn't give you the best feeling, frankly, when you turn on the news and every day there is a different cyber attack.

And sophisticated banks and Fintechs are using AI-based tools to verify information using multiple massive data sets instead of government-required info. Can you speak just from a cybercrime standpoint what the move to digital ID in the United States can get us?

Mr. GRANT. I think it makes it a lot harder for the attackers who are exploiting what in some cases is nonexistent digital identity infrastructure or legacy tools that worked a few years ago, but that the attackers have caught up with. And so, much of what I think about when it comes, not just with identity, but anything when it comes to cybercrime and cybersecurity is, how do you prevent scaleable attacks? How do you raise the cost of attacks so that it is not easy for an attacker to do, frankly, what we have seen in banking or government benefits over the last year at the slightest through-some of these systems?

I think the more you know, whether it is looking at some of the deterministic factors we can bring in with what Chairman Foster's bill would do, in terms of being able to ask an agency to vouch for you, just like you can use your card in the paper world. How do you use it digitally? How do you augment that with AI as well to try and—I think I had mentioned before Congresswoman Adams had asked, how was used AI used. AI can study how criminal rings do things and look for telltale signs.

Putting those together, we are in a bit of an arm's race against increasingly organized criminal gangs. They are starting to use AI as well. I think we are going to need, unfortunately, every weapon at our disposal to guard against these increasingly sophisticated attacks.

Mr. GONZALEZ OF OHIO. Thank you. Mr. Fredung, same question. From a cybersecurity and a protection standpoint, what does moving toward digital ID do for your average American?

Mr. FREDUNG. Yes, thank you Congressman. First of all, I would like to follow up with what Jeremy mentioned in regards to staying ahead of the more sophisticated sources as well. For what we are seeing in space like the east attacks by sharing information on the government, this is pretty much easy for companies such as ourselves to prevent our assets. The more sophisticated ones using, let's say, EID phase, for example, those are the tougher ones to essentially track down.

Switching from we used to refer to as data elevation—I think you mentioned in regards to the social security number, or I think a list but also mentioned in regards to the other corridor was checking quality information from one individual against the database.

That is quite out-aged to be completely honest, because anybody can steal anybody else's information. And government databases don't give you a particularly accurate assault. So by moving towards more of the identification which combines facial documentation alongside biometric identification, it is definitely, in our experience, the way to move ahead.

Mr. GONZALEZ OF OHIO. Thank you. Mr. Chairman, I yield back. I have no more questions.

Chairman FOSTER. Thank you, and we will now recognize Mr. Casten for 5 minutes.

Mr. CASTEN. Thank you. And I am glad we have the second round, because I ran out of time with Professor Renieris. I want to follow up, and I want pick up on some stuff that I think you alluded to with Mr. Budd and Mr. Auchincloss.

There are few advantages of blockchain and distributive ledger technology, more broadly, as far as, obviously, creating a record of this digital ID where it is and making sure there is some integrity to the data that stores it. There is also, as we have seen in the crypto space, the potential for the anonymity that comes from to be abused.

And so, I guess I have a two-part question. Number one, are you satisfied that blockchain is the right technology to store the data around a digital ID? And let me just hear your answer to that before I go to the second question.

Ms. RENIERIS. Thank you for the question, Congressman. I list in my written testimony and quite explicitly point out that I think blockchain is actually the wrong technology for personal identity management. I have a lot of experience in that space. I have worked directly in-house with blockchain start-ups. I worked with many of my own people since the various intergovernmental groups on this.

Blockchain is inherently an accounting technology. Its features are transparency, auditability, traceability, and permanence for mutability. Those are things that you might want to use, for example, for supply chain management, but they are really not things that you want to use for personal identity management if you are concerned about the privacy and security of individuals.

Over the last 4 to 5 years, as I have been part of these conversations with governments and industry, there have been many, many technical solutions proposed to get around some of the concerns, a lot of different pseudonymization and anonymization techniques, a lot of different methods of encryption. But, conceptionally—and at the heart of what blockchain does and what it is designed to do is really at odds with poor data protection principals around things like data minimization.

For example, if I want to prove who I am, I don't want that data replicated across nodes around the world. If I do that, I don't know if the data is stored indefinitely.

So really, to me, it is a complete misfit between the purpose you are trying to achieve, but I know you have more questions.

Mr. CASTEN. That is helpful. The reason I tied this to my earlier question is because, in my head at least, this is tied to, is there going to be a privately-owned for-profit digital ID that is going to get out ahead of us? Because the value of that data—there is the narrow part of my biometrics, that this is me and I know this is you. And then, there is all of the metadata around it, which is, of course, where the money is. Right? Who are you connected to? Where was the GPS tied when you used your ID? What did you use your ID for, et cetera, et cetera?

However we store this—and I will stipulate that you have an idea in your head about where we should store this digital ID— should we also be using that same place as a repository for that metadata? Where should that metadata live, because someone is going to use it, and what are your thoughts on that?

Ms. RENIERIS. Yes, it is a really important point to make. And I think that sophisticated for blockchain—teams working on this have recognized that it is really a bad idea to store the actual identity credentials on the ledger, so they have come up with workarounds for that. But ultimately the ledger of the blockchain is a record of the metadata that you are describing, the transactional data.

And I think a really important thing that is very overlooked in this conversation is that the commercial incentives I was talking about in the business model, the revenue models here can really undo a lot of the technical features intended to provide privacy and anonymity.

For example, of a lot of the blockchain-enabled identity schemes, really lacked a business model. And a common one that is proposed is a kind of scheme where the verifying party pays the issuer of the credential when that credential is used to kind of recoup some of the costs of issuing the credential.

When you have that kind of scheme where you pay for verification, ultimately, you have to be able to separate the accounting and the transactions. And that is actually a more sophisticated problem to solve. And a lot of companies I have seen in this space have thought about it, if they even thought about the question. And so, again, even if you use best sort of encryption technologies or anonymization techniques in place, you might have a business model that undoes all of the benefits of the technology.

Mr. CASTEN. I realize we are out of time, and maybe this is a longer conversation, but if I take my government-issued passport right now, that has a whole lot of metadata in it. It has the date of issue, it has where I have traveled, it is all information. And there is some value to governments of having that information like my birth certificate or anything else.

If we do a perfect government digital ID, should we be collecting and accumulating that metadata if we get into privacy issues and all of the rest of that? Somehow, we have to solve that, right? And I realize I am out of time, but you are welcome to respond.

Ms. RENIERIS. I think the question is, to what end and for what purposes? And I think those would have to be explicitly stated upfront. This is something I also alluded to in my written testimony. And I am happy to provide more feedback on the record.

Mr. CASTEN. Thank you. I yield back.

Chairman FOSTER. You could possibly implement a witness protection program using a blockchain-enabled ID, which is essentially government-sponsored identity fraud.

We will now recognize Mr. Taylor for 5 minutes.

Mr. TAYLOR. Thank you Mr. Chairman. Mr. Casten, I think if you go back to last year, Professor Renieris actually resigned from the ID 2020 project, objecting to blockchain. So, you actually asked the exact right person about blockchain and identity.

And it was a really fascinating conversation, Representative Casten. Would you like to take 60 seconds to kind of continue down this rabbit hole?

Mr. CASTEN. Oh, you are very kind. I will defer to your time. Maybe we can just follow up. Maybe we can set up a time for the three of us, if you would like, to get together when we are not watching the clock. I appreciate it.

Mr. TAYLOR. Sure. I appreciate your passion for this particular topic and the importance you feel of not using blockchain technology for identification.

Just going back down kind of the horror story, it is really instructive to me to know what not to do, as well as sort of what to do.

Dr. Maynard-Atem, I know in your written testimony you talked about, I believe, the health system in Kenya, women's ability to access that because of the identification system they put in place. Do you want to expand with on what you have seen in terms of how not to do it or how we shouldn't do it in a digital identification system?

Ms. MAYNARD-ATEM. Absolutely. Thank you for the question, Congressman. I think in my written testimony, I do share a little bit of the horror stories or the ways that it has gone wrong. And a lot of that comes from—and I think Professor Renieris mentioned this previously—not taking into account who your actual users are, and not taking into account what it is that they are trying to achieve with digital identities and any solutions that are put in place.

In the instance in Kenya that I referenced, lots of people in that particular market, women don't tend to have access to the required documents or mobile phones, et cetera, to allow them to make their way through the process of obtaining a digital identity.

If I think about examples here in the UK, a lot of the digital identities previously and the schemes have been tried have been relied on having certain documents or access to the internet, for example. And I think it is 20 percent—but don't quote me on that— of the UK who don't have those government-issued documents.

So if your predication of digital identity is based off of having access to particular things, whether that is documents or whether that is a mobile phone, et cetera, then automatically you are excluding X percentage of your entire population that you are designed to serve.

I think the requirements gathering the start of all of these exercises needs to take into account the different situations that people are in, and you need to be able to account for those different situations.

So, yes, all of us on this call clearly have access to technology and government-issued IDs, but we need to be thinking about the people who don'thave access to those things or who might not be able to access those things, those people who can't necessarily use technology to get to the systems that they need to, to get to the services that they need.

I think it all starts at the very beginning of the process and being able to identify all of the different use cases that you are trying to serve, rather than just the most common use cases that you can satisfy the majority of people. We need to take into account all of those differences and make sure we are accounting for those in the solution that we produce.

Mr. TAYLOR. Professor Renieris, just getting back to you, you touched briefly on India in my prior question. Could you just talk a little bit about how, in your mind, India went wrong? I think that is—I don't want to put words in your mouth. I recall that phrase by you.

Ms. RENIERIS. Sure. I think the situation with Aadhaar in India is—there are a couple of places where they went wrong. First, they intended this single unique identifier and the system to apply to every aspect of life.

So, there is literally nothing you can access without using it. And it is entirely traceable across all of these facets of life by the government. The constitutional court subsequently looked into this and specifically said that it was an overreach and that there are concerns about dialing some of that back.

But in terms of the questions surrounding inclusion, that was also the concern there, because of the complexity of India and because of the complexity of the population, everything from different languages to different cultures to very different infrastructure in different regions in the country, there wasn't enough consideration around how groups might be impacted in that respect and how they might be excluded.

I think we have a very similar problem here. You talked about broadband earlier in the hearing where we don't have a homogenous population, we don't have universal access to things.

And if we sort of, as Dr. Maynard-Atem said, if we only solve for the majority, then for the tyranny majority there and we don't have the pluralism and pluralistic perspective we need to design a system that is actually inclusive in the works for most people.

Mr. TAYLOR. Thank you. I appreciate that, Professor.

Mr. Chairman, I yield back.

Chairman FOSTER. Thank you. And we will, finally, recognize Representative Adams for 5 minutes.

Ms. ADAMS. Thank you, Mr. Chairman. Cyber attacks are the fastest-growing crime in the U.S., and one of the largest threats to the data in the electronic infrastructure today. Studies have predicted that the business world fall victim to ransomware every 11 seconds this year. A centralized digital ID base with people's personal information would be a huge target.

So, Mr. Kelts, can you discuss the cryptography and the smartphone techniques available so that there would be no need for a central digital ID database?

Mr. KELTS. Yes. I think that there are multiple different architectures that can support what you are referring to and not have any centralized database. In the mobile driver's license, there are opportunities to take that data and put it onto the smartphone itself, along with the cryptographic signatures so that when that data is shared, selectively shared, the signatures can be shared with it, and the verifier can take the signatures and check on that data.

I think there are other architectures similar to that. And I actually think that is something I can distribute a ledger or blockchain that holds caches, has that capability if I have the data. And if I present it to you as a business or verifier of the data, you can then go and check the veracity of that data.

In addition to non-centralized databases, having access to verifiable data, cryptographically-verifiable data can reduce the need for businesses themselves to store the end result, because they know the next time that person comes along, they will get fresher, newer validated data, and they don't have to keep large records. I think that has the potential also to reduce not just centralized databases, but peripheral databases that are also the targets of that.

Ms. ADAMS. Right. Thank you very much, Mr. Chairman. I have no further questions. I yield back.

Chairman FOSTER. Thank you. And I would like to thank our witnesses for their testimony today.

The Chair notes that some Members may have additional questions for these witnesses, which they may wish to submit in writing. Without objection, the hearing record will remain open for 5 legislative days for Members to submit written questions to these witnesses and to place their responses in the record. Also, without objection, Members will have 5 legislative days to submit extraneous materials to the Chair for inclusion in the record.

And with that, this hearing is adjourned.

[Whereupon, at 1:40 p.m., the hearing was adjourned.]

Written Testimony of Victor Fredung, Chief Executive Officer, Shufti Pro, before the House Financial Services Committee, Task Force on Artificial Intelligence, Hearing on I Am Who I Say I Am: Verifying Identity while Preserving Privacy in the Digital Age, Friday, July 16, 2021

Chairman Foster, Ranking Member Gonzalez, and distinguished members of the Committee. Thank you for inviting me to testify before you today on this very important topic.

My name is Victor Fredung and I am the Chief Executive Officer and Co-Founder at Shufti Pro. Shufti Pro is a SaaS provider offering AI-powered identity verification services. We offer KYC verification and AML screening solutions to multiple industries including but not limited to; banks, financial institutions, exchanges, P2P, travel, healthcare, gaming and crypto firms in over 230+ countries and territories. Our state of the art IDV services empower businesses to unveil the true identity of their customers and end-users before onboarding them or allowing access to services. I'm very glad to be a part of this discussion and to speak about the significance of AI in identity verification.

Identity fraud is on the rise, as per the latest reports of FTC. According to the Aite Group, 47 percent of Americans experienced financial identity theft in 2020. The group's report, U.S. Identity Theft: The Stark Reality, found that losses from identity theft cases cost $502.5 billion in 2019 and increased 42 percent to $712.4 billion in 2020. Shufti Pro's mission is to build a safe online environment, devoid of identity frauds, by making IDV seamless and 100% accurate to fight multifaceted fraud in real-time. We serve financial businesses, facilitating them to stay compliant with the latest KYC/AML regulatory developments. As the digital ecosystem grows, it is important that businesses and customers have confidence in it.

Today, I would like to discuss:

1. How identity theft is becoming a more serious crime since more people go online (covid spike)
2. How does our AI perform highly accurate verifications? How do we train our models?
3. Detecting tampered ID documents through AI-powered anti-spoofing measures.
4. Preventing identity theft with automated IDV and liveness checks
5. The challenge of data privacy in online identity verification
6. How using automated identity verification gives a higher accuracy and a more seamless user-experience
7. How Shufti Pro can help governments and businesses streamline onboarding and verification of customers

I would like to note that while the focus of today's hearing is identity verification. While fake documents and spoofing attacks are some examples of how criminals try to bypass ID checks, the majority of customers are legitimate. The major task is to integrate the advanced technology that can differentiate the compromised identities from the real ones. In 2020, Shufti Pro encountered a 3.36% rise in global identity fraud as compared to 2019. I'm afraid 2020's reported illicit activities will rise this year as with time we'll learn more about scams and frauds that have not been identified yet.

How Identity Theft Is Becoming a More Serious Crime Since More People Started Going Online

Year 2020 has been a year of transformation. With the emergence of COVID-19 pandemic, businesses have gone remote, shifting major operations to the digital sphere. This has provided an opportunity for cybercriminals to exploit businesses using fake identities. Over the past few months, multiple data breaches have exposed billions of personal, financial and healthcare records, resulting in identity frauds. There's a high possibility that the intensity of these frauds will increase in upcoming years.

According to the FTC, the cases of identity theft in the United States doubled in 2020 as cybercriminals started taking advantage of the COVID-relief benefits offered by the government to the public. These stats are officially announced by the FTC on their website during annual 'Identity Theft Awareness Week', in which they received about 1.4 million reports of identity theft last year. Most of the cybercriminals were targeting the government funds embarked to facilitate unemployed citizens. There were 394,280 government benefits fraud reports as compared to 12,900 reports in 2019. Such frauds involved imposters filing for unemployment benefits due to the ongoing pandemic. In fact, according to Shufti Pro's annual fraud report, the biometric fraud rate in the US was approx. 12% higher in 2020 than 2019.

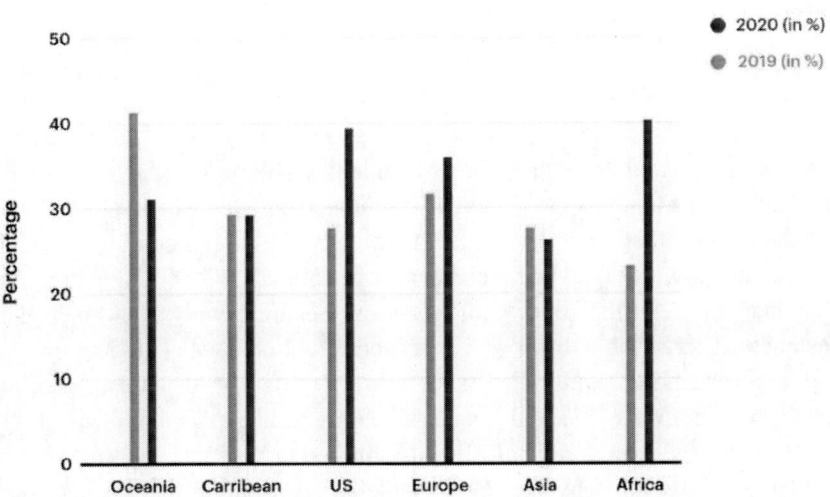

This is not it, we believe this year we'll witness even more cases of identity theft. For fraudsters will become more versed in adopting sophisticated technologies to fulfill their malicious intents. In order to combat them, businesses need even more intelligent verification solutions that can unveil the true identity of an individual within seconds and that too leaving no room for false positives.

How Does Our AI Perform Highly Accurate Verifications? How Do We Train Our Models?

KYC for Customer Onboarding - The Process

| Customer Registration | End-user uploads ID Document | Data extraction through OCR | Face Verification | Background Checks | KYC Checklist Fulfilled | Customer Onboarded |

Source: Shufti Pro

Shufti Pro's configurable IDV solutions incorporate enhanced AI technology to accurately verify the user's identity online. We train our systems by deploying thousands of AI models. We understand the risk associated with false positives, that's why at Shufti Pro we ensure that our continual models are enhanced with every new verification performed. It's an understood fact that machine learning algorithms get more accurate with every new data instance. That's the reason we incorporate AI and ML models in our verification engine. Shufti Pro takes pride in offering an industry-leading accuracy rate of 98.67%. And it's possible only because of our enhanced AI.

Businesses similar to Shufti Pro use limited or test data to train their AI models. The reason why they are unable to achieve the highest accuracy. Whereas in case of our AI, we assure to deploy continual ML models that incorporate real-time data. Not only this, but Shufti Pro synergizes human intelligence as well to back the results generated through AI. This reduces the chances of false positives and facilitates training highly efficient models. Unlike other service providers, we make sure the customer is only verified if all the ID checks are adequately met; for instance, ID document is valid and not expired, data is not forged, document template is accurate, checking for rainbow prints, holograms etc. and verifying the MRZ code as well.

Detecting Tampered ID Documents through AI-Powered Anti-Spoofing Measures

We all witness people using fake ID documents at some point, for instance teenagers using them to enter the club, adults using them to file for government relief programs etc. In the digital space, using fake or stolen ID documents has become more than common. Though businesses have started incorporating IDV checks to authenticate users before allowing access to online services or onboarding them, the majority of these checks are not capable enough to catch the spoof attempts. Tampering with identity documents and creating fake or synthetic ID documents are the most common strategies that imposters use to bypass identity verification checks.

Criminals these days are technologically advanced and ensure to tamper the documents in such a way that makes them almost undetected. But all thanks to AI-powered anti-spoofing measures that are specifically designed to identify professionally forged or synthetic documents. We utilize various anti-spoofing techniques to detect tampered documents, and that too within a fraction of seconds; no long waits!

With techniques such as pixel detection, filtering lights, hologram detection, our AI-powered identity verification engine can seamlessly detect any manipulations done to a document. For instance, if a criminal photoshops the date of birth on the ID document, through pixel detection technique, it can be identified. Moreover, our system also reads the data from the MRZ code and that data is matched against the information printed on the ID card to check for any manipulations.

These are few ID card manipulations that Shufti Pro encountered while verifying ID documents in 2020.

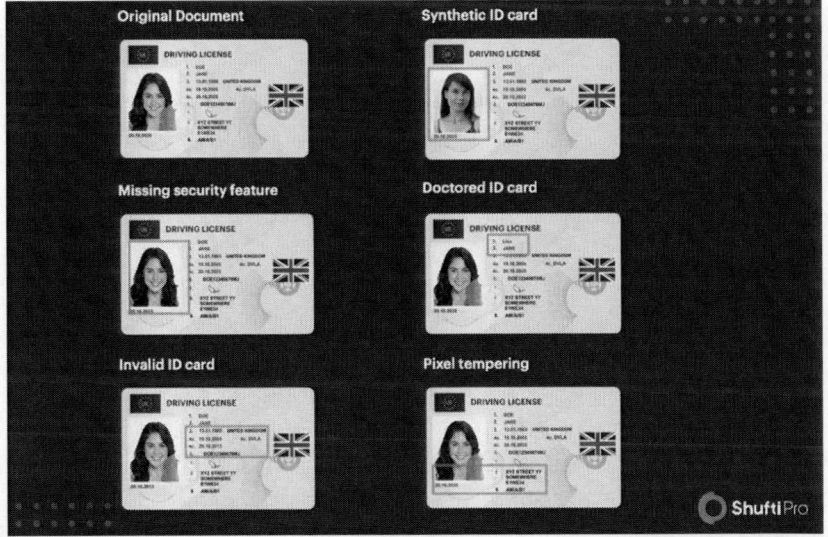

In 2020, over 19% of the document verifications performed by Shufti Pro were flagged because fake, doctored, stolen or synthetic identity documents were submitted during the identity verification process. And this year, we believe these stats to rise.

Preventing Identity Theft with Automated IDV and Liveness Checks

While criminals have developed sophisticated methods of messing with identity documents, biometrics are still considered secure for ID authentication. Criminals are adopting new ways to spoof biometric verification tools. We believe these spoof attempts can be prevented with our automated IDV solution incorporating 3D liveness checks. Many times, criminals try various facial spoof attacks, such as 2D and 3D masks, eye-cut photos, screenshots, and video replays. The majority of biometric fraud attempts captured by Shufti Pro in 2020 were 2D and 3D spoof attempts. The end-user either displayed a paper-backed photo or took a photo from the screen of another device.

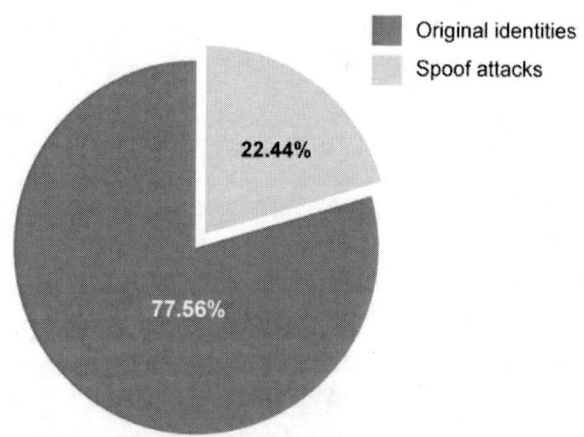

Out of all verifications performed by Shufti Pro in 2020, over 22% of them were biometric fraud attempts.

Automated IDV leverages 3D liveness checks such as 3D-depth perception, micro-expression analysis, 3D AI mapping etc. By using 3D mapping, Shufti Pro detects the 3D angles and minor facial movements to ensure the presence of a real person. It ensures to check for relevant markers for liveness detection. Those relative markers consist of checks for eyes, skin texture, photoshop, age and hair colour differences. Its deep machine learning algorithm makes sure optimal micro expression analysis is conducted through adequate data comparison. Referring to a computational algorithm, various points on the picture are matched to that of a previously digitized template. Shufti Pro's liveness detection shows an individual's live presence and prevents facial spoof attacks as well.

The Challenge of Data Privacy in Online ID Verification

Whenever asked for proof of identity or age, be it a driving license, ID card or a passport, we present a wealth of personal information; for instance, name, date of birth, address, signature, etc. In this age, data is a goldmine for cybercriminals. User's information, if gone in wrong hands, can cause destruction not just for individuals but the businesses as well. Data breaches are common in the digital world. In 2020, 75% of large companies in the UK reported data breaches. The global pandemic has witnessed the surge in personal information online as more and more businesses are shifting their operations online and people are turning to these services in turn.

However, the majority of the people are still reluctant in adopting digital identities and getting themselves verified digitally. Even though we all know that signing up for a new bank from the comfort of home is much more convenient and quick with real-time ID verification. The concern for data privacy and protection is what's hindering digital IDV to become widespread. Keeping this concern as our priority, our AI-powered ID verification solutions strictly follow data privacy standards to secure consumer's data. Using the services offered by Shufti Pro, our clients' end-users can have complete control over their data. We are GDPR and PCI-DSS compliant, following proper data encryption and security standards.

How Using Automated Identity Verification Gives a Higher Accuracy and a More Seamless User-Experience

Customers are the true assets of any company, and customer experience plays a vital role in defining the customer-business relationship. Over 60% of US consumers prefer an automated self-service, such as a website or mobile app, for simple customer service tasks. We at Shufti Pro strive hard to offer a great customer experience to boost customer acquisition. With automated identity verification in place, customers don't need to put manual effort and wait for days and weeks to get their identity verified. All AI-powered IDV tools required is for the customer to show their face and identity document in the camera and the system does the rest. Unlike traditional verification models, the automated ID verification system by Shufti Pro utilizes intelligent OCR technology to automatically extract data from the document, and performs verification real-quick. This leaves no room for human glitch and the higher accuracy is assured. Moreover, we synergize human and artificial intelligence to reduce any chances of false positives.

How Shufti Pro Can Help Governments and Businesses Streamline Onboarding and Verification of Customers

Living in the digital world, the current legacy solutions used by the government institutions to verify user identities and combat identity thieves are falling short. And some digital solutions require users to upload scanned copies of their identity documents and wait till the experts on the other end verify them manually. This can be time-consuming and tedious. Moreover, storing personally identifiable information (PII) in one location can raise security and privacy concerns due to ever-growing data breach incidents. Not to forget that these identity documents can be forged or manipulated that are most of the time unidentifiable. Government agencies need to implement intelligent digital IDV solutions that are developed using AI and ML models and follow strict data privacy guidelines. That's where Shufti Pro comes in.

With Shufti Pro's identity verification solution on the frontend, government agencies can provide fast and secure checks to allow access to services and combat the massive identity fraud. We utilize artificial intelligence to provide a sophisticated and frictionless workflow that would not only authenticate the individual's identity but also identify the risks associated with the user-claimed identity in real-time through screening against 1700+ global watchlists, sanctions and PEPs.

Moreover, we understand the importance of consumer data, that's why we offer an on-premises identity verification solution that you can host over your own servers and have complete control over the consumer data.

Jeremy Grant, Coordinator, the Better Identity Coalition, U.S. House Financial Services Committee, Task Force on Artificial Intelligence, "I Am Who I Say I Am: Verifying Identity while Preserving Privacy in the Digital Age," July 16, 2021

Chairman Foster, Ranking Member Gonzalez and members of the committee, thank you for the opportunity to discuss the topic of identity verification with you today.

I am here today on behalf of the Better Identity Coalition[1] – an organization launched in 2018 focused on bringing together leading firms from different sectors to develop a set of consensus, cross-sector policy recommendations that promote the adoption of better solutions for identity verification and authentication. The Coalition's founding members include recognized leaders from diverse sectors of the economy, including financial services, health care, technology, FinTech, payments, and security.

Up front, I want to flag that the Better Identity Coalition is not seeking to push the interests of any one technology or industry. Instead, our members are united by a common recognition that the way we handle identity today in the U.S. is broken – and by a common desire to see both the public and private sectors each take steps to make identity systems work better. It's very fitting that the Task Force has called this hearing in this particular week, as it's one that marks the three-year anniversary of our publication of "Better Identity in America: A Blueprint for Policymakers" – laying out five key initiatives that government should launch around identity that are both meaningful in impact and practical to implement. And as I will discuss today, the need for government action here is greater than ever.

As background, I've worked for more than 20 years at the intersection of identity and cybersecurity. Over the course of my career, I've been a Senate staffer, led a business unit at a technology company architecting and building digital identity systems, and done stints at two investment banks helping investors understand the identity market – cutting through what works and what doesn't, and where they should put capital. In 2011, I was selected to lead the National Strategy for Trusted Identities in Cyberspace (NSTIC), a White House initiative focused on improving security, privacy, choice and innovation online through better approaches to digital identity. In that role I

---

[1] More on the Better Identity Coalition can be found at https://www.betteridentity.org.

worked with industry and government to tackle major challenges in identity, built out what is now the Trusted Identities Group at the National Institute of Standards and Technology (NIST), and also served as NIST's Senior Executive Advisor for Identity Management. I left government in 2015 and now lead the Technology Business Strategy practice at Venable, a law firm with the country's leading privacy and cybersecurity practice. In my role at Venable I serve as the Coordinator of the Better Identity Coalition.

I will cover three core topics in my testimony today:

1. First, I will set the stage by detailing some of the problems with our existing approach to identity verification – and the enormous costs they present.
2. Second, I will discuss how these problems can be solved – looking at the question of "What should government and industry do about identity now?" I'll explain why government – as the only authoritative issuer of identity – must play a role in the solution, and how doing so can help to spur not just improvements in security, but also economic growth. Chairman Foster's recently introduced "Improving Digital Identity Act of 2021" is critical here.
3. Third, given that this hearing is in the Artificial Intelligence (AI) Taskforce, I will discuss the role of AI and Machine Learning (ML) in identity verification – looking at how these technologies being used to deliver better identity outcomes, as well as identifying potential risks, and ways to mitigate those risks.

Setting the Stage

Let me say up front that I am grateful to the Committee's AI Task Force for calling this hearing today, as well as to Chairman Foster for his leadership on this topic. The legislation that he and Congressmen Katko, Langevin and Loudermilk introduced two weeks ago – "The Improving Digital Identity Act of 2021" – is the single most important policy initiative the government can undertake to address the inadequacies of America's identity infrastructure.

At a high level, that should be one of the top takeaways for members of this Task Force today – identity is critical infrastructure and needs to be treated as such. DHS said as much in 2019 when it declared identity as one of 55 "National Critical Functions," defined as those services "so vital to the United States that their disruption, corruption, or dysfunction would have a debilitating effect on security, national economic security, national public health or safety, or any combination thereof."[2] Despite this designation, identity has gotten scant investment and attention. The Improving Digital Identity Act, if approved, will get us started.

And we are overdue to get started! The way we handle identity in America impacts our security, our privacy, and our liberty. And from an economic standpoint, particularly as we move high-value transactions into the digital world, identity can be the great enabler – providing a foundation for digital transactions and online experiences that are more secure, more enjoyable for the user, and ideally, more respectful of their privacy.

But when we don't get identity right, we enable a set of great attack points for criminals and other adversaries looking to execute attacks in cyberspace. And with it, we end up creating new burdens for consumers, businesses, and government agencies who need to accurately verify identity to enable high value transactions to be delivered online.

This was already a problem when this Task Force last convened nearly two years ago to consider digital identity, but the enormity of the problem has been magnified several times over the last 18 months amidst a pandemic that literally made it impossible to engage in most in-person transactions. The pandemic laid bare the inadequacies of the nation's digital identity infrastructure – enabling cybercriminals to steal billions of dollars and creating major barriers for Americans trying to obtain critical benefits and services.

More than $63 billion was stolen from state unemployment insurance (UI) programs by cybercriminals exploiting weak identity verification and authentication systems, according to the Labor Department's Inspector General. On the flip side, we've seen hundreds of stories about Americans who are out of work because of the pandemic, and who have been unable to get the UI benefits that they desperately need, because their application has been falsely flagged for "fraud" when they are unable to successfully navigate the convoluted, labyrinthine processes many states have put in place to verify identity.

Beyond UI, the inadequacy of our identity infrastructure remains a major challenge in financial services: FinCEN last year reported banks are losing more than $1 billion each month due to identity-related cybercrime.[3] Meanwhile, millions of Americans cannot get a bank account because they

---

[2] See https://www.cisa.gov/national-critical-functions-set.
[3] Per FinCEN at the 2020 Federal Identity Forum.

don't have the foundational identity documents needed to prove who they are. Amidst all of this, identity theft losses soared by 42% last year.[4]

On the cybersecurity front, it remains an anomaly when a major incident occurs and identity does not provide the attack vector. The SolarWinds attack several months ago was just the latest example of this, with Russian attackers targeting the administrative layer of identity and access management systems to do devastating damage.

As a leader at the Cybersecurity and Infrastructure Security Agency (CISA) at the Department of Homeland Security stated back in March, "Identity is everything now."[5]

Why are there so many problems here? A key takeaway for this Committee to understand today is that attackers have caught up with many of the "first-generation tools" we have used to protect, verify and authenticate identity. Recent incidents may have driven this point home, but the reality is that these tools have been vulnerable for quite some time. There are many reasons for this – and certainly blame to allocate – but the most important question is:

What Should Government and Industry Do About It Now?

That's a key point – government and industry. If there is one message this Committee should take away from today's hearing, it's that industry has said they cannot solve this alone. We are at a juncture where the government will need to step up and play a bigger role to help address critical vulnerabilities in our "digital identity fabric." Passing the Improving Digital Identity Act is where we should start.

Let me say a few words about that bill: I've been asked quite a few times over the last year, "How do we fix identity verification in state unemployment systems?" or "How do we fix identity in banking?" or health care or government services? The answer is simple: you can't. In that identity is a national issue, and the core problems are the same for most every use case. Anyone trying to focus on "solving identity" for a particular use case, while well-meaning, is going to fail.

---

[4] See https://aitegroup.com/report/us-identity-theft-stark-reality.
[5] See https://federalnewsnetwork.com/cybersecurity/2021/03/cisa-identity-is-everything-for-cyber-defense-post-solarwinds/.

The good news is that these problems are not insurmountable. The U.S. can address its shortcomings by investing in creating "Digital First" identity infrastructure that leverages our existing nationally recognized, authoritative identity systems to create digital counterparts to the paper and plastic IDs they issue today. The Improving Digital Identity Act will do just that, and it is a critical piece of legislation.

In terms of level setting, it might be helpful to define "what we're talking about when we talk about digital identity." In that the term "identity" is thrown around a lot and used in a lot of different ways.

Fundamentally, there are two core challenges we are trying to solve.

1. The first is figuring out whether someone is who they claim to be at account opening – what's generally called "identity proofing." Exploiting weaknesses in our identity proofing infrastructure is what has allowed criminals to steal tens of billions of dollars from state UI programs, as well as financial services firms.
2. And second is "authentication." Once an account has been created – how you create systems that can securely log customers in to that account? This has become quite important in a world where passwords just don't cut it anymore, and cybercriminals are exploiting the weaknesses of passwords and other weak authentication tools to launch billions of attacks each day.

Here, the challenges faced by the market are not the same. I made a point two years ago that I will make again today, which is that across the identity marketplace: Authentication is getting easier, but Identity Proofing is getting harder.

Authentication Is Getting Easier, but Identity Proofing Is Getting Harder

Let me unpack that first part: Authentication is getting easier. By that, I mean that while passwords are broken, the ability of consumers and businesses to access tools that they can use in addition to – or in lieu of – passwords is greater than it's ever been. And with multi-stakeholder industry initiatives like the FIDO Alliance creating next-generation multi-factor authentication (MFA) standards that are getting baked into most devices, browsers and operating systems, it is becoming easier than ever to deliver on the vision of better security, privacy and convenience. Microsoft, Google and Apple all support the FIDO standards via built-in support in Windows, Android, iOS and macOS, meaning it's hard for someone to buy a device these days that does not support FIDO authentication out of the box. This, in turn, is making it easier than ever for firms in financial services and other sectors to deliver passwordless experiences. The development and adoption of the FIDO standards is, in my view, the most significant development in the authentication marketplace in the last 20 years. I expect FIDO authentication to also play a big role in the Federal government's efforts to comply with the Biden Administration's recent Executive Order mandate for universal MFA across all government systems, helping to fill in the gaps where the government's legacy, PKI-based smart card authentication tools cannot easily do the job.

By pairing new authentication standards like FIDO with analytics solutions that use AI and ML to "score" in real time the likelihood that an account remains in the hands of its rightful owner, we are closer than ever to eliminating reliance on passwords.

But while Authentication is getting easier – Identity Proofing is getting harder. By that, I mean the ability of consumers during initial account creation to prove that they are who they really claim to be is harder than ever – in part because attackers have caught up to the tools we have depended on for identity proofing and verification.

This means that it is harder than ever for businesses and government – as more transactions move online – to verify someone's identity when someone is creating an account or applying for a new service. Better tools are needed here. But unlike with passwords – where the market has responded with tools like FIDO authentication and behavior analytics to fix the problem – the market has not yet sorted things out here. To be clear, there is great industry innovation in the identity proofing space, including by many of the Coalition's members. But the one thing that has become clear in discussion with industry is that the private sector cannot solve this problem on its own.

Why is that? Well, as one of our members noted, the title of this hearing – "I am who I say I am" – is technically incorrect, since for all purposes, when it comes to identity, you are who the government says you are. One might ask the government to recognize a name change if you want to go by a different name – an Iowa man named Jeffrey Wilschke famously changed his name several years ago to Beezow Doo-doo Zopittybop-bop-bop[6] – but it's safe to say his bank, the DMV, the TSA, the IRS, the SSA, his health insurer, and dozens of other parties he engages with would not be willing to recognize that name had the government not first done so.

This point really gets to the heart of the issue when it comes to identity proofing: At the end of the day, government is the only authoritative issuer of identity in the United States. But the identity systems government administers are largely stuck in the paper world, whereas commerce has increasingly moved online. This "identity gap" – a complete absence of credentials built to support digital transactions – is being actively exploited by adversaries to steal identities, money and sensitive data, and defraud consumers, governments, and businesses alike.

A core challenge here is that adversaries have caught up with the systems America has used for remote identity proofing and verification. Many of these systems were developed to fill the "identity gap" in the U.S. caused by the lack of any formal digital identity system – for example, Knowledge-Based Verification (KBV) systems that attempt to verify identity online by asking applicants several questions that, in theory, only they should be able to answer. Now that adversaries, through multiple breaches, have obtained enough data to defeat many KBV systems; the answers that were once secret are now commonly known. Next generation solutions are needed that are not only more resilient, but also more convenient for consumers.

Industry is innovating here, and AI-enabled solutions are one of the tools that can help. But they alone are not enough. The single best way to address the weaknesses of KBV and other first-generation identity verification tools is for the government to fill the "identity gap" that led to their creation. This idea is at the heart of the Better Identity Coalition's key recommendations for how government and the private sector can improve the identity ecosystem, as well as the Improving Digital Identity Act.

It's an idea that eschews the tired, old idea of trying to solve problems with a national ID card. The reality is that we don't need new identity systems – and part of our problem is that we have too many cards today, another one will not help. Instead, we need to leverage the authoritative government identity systems that we already have at the Federal, state and local level, but

---

[6] More on Mr. Doo-doo Zopittybop-bop-bop and his journey is at https://madison.com/wsj/news/local/beezow-doo-doo-zopittybop-bop-bop-behind-the-name-a-complex-figure/article_14ccf4aa-87f6-11e1-83e2-0019bb2963f4.html.

that are largely stuck in the paper world; none of them can be easily used – or validated – online.

The inability to do so today means that consumers are hamstrung if they need to prove their identity – or certain attributes about themselves – online, in that they are unable to use the credentials sitting in their pockets and wallets. It increases risk for both consumers and the parties they seek to transact with.

To fix this, America's paper-based systems should be modernized around a privacy-protecting, consumer-centric model that allows consumers to ask the government agency that issued a credential to stand behind it in the online world – by validating the information from the credential.

The creation of "Government Attribute Validation Services" can help to transform legacy identity verification processes and help consumers and businesses alike improve trust online.

Such services could be offered by an agency itself, or through accredited, privately run "gateway service providers" that would administer these services and facilitate connections between consumers, online services providers, and governments.

The Social Security Administration (SSA) and state governments – the latter in their role as issuers of driver's licenses and identity cards – are the best positioned entities to offer these services to consumers.

Indeed, the SSA has built just the sort of Attribute Validation Service that we called for, the Electronic Consent Based Social Security Number Verification (eCBSV) Service. SSA is doing so in response to Section 215 of the Economic Growth, Regulatory Relief, and Consumer Protection Act, which was signed into law in 2018 thanks, in part, to this Committee's work.

The eCBSV system now allows financial institutions and their service providers to electronically get a "Yes/No" answer as to whether an individual's SSN, name, and date of birth combination matches Social Security records. We're thrilled to see SSA lead the way here.

First, because eCBSV will change the game in the fight against synthetic identity fraud, which costs the country $6-$8 billion annually. The fact that fraudsters have been targeting the SSNs of children to commit this fraud is especially galling – eCBSV has given the country a tool to fight back.

And second, because what SSA is doing here provides a template for other agencies.

The Improving Digital Identity Act would jumpstart the creation of similar services at the Federal, State and Local level through four core initiatives:

- First, it would state that it is the policy of the U.S. Government to use its authorities and capabilities to enhance the security, reliability, privacy, and convenience of digital identity solutions that support and protect transactions between individuals, government entities, and businesses, and that enable Americans to prove who they are online. With this, the bill would set up a formal, White-House led "Improving Digital Identity Task Force" charged with bringing together key Federal, state, and local agencies who all issue identity credentials to develop secure methods for government agencies to validate identity attributes in a way that protects the privacy and security of individuals, and supports reliable, interoperable digital identity verification tools in the public and private sectors.

  The focus on bringing Federal, state, and local governments together is essential, given that America's authoritative identity systems are split between all these levels of government. For example, my birth certificate was issued by the county I was born in, my driver's license is issued by my state DMV, and my passport was issued by the State Department. I should be able to ask any of those organizations to vouch for me when I am trying to prove who I am online – in a way that is standards-based, offers a consistent user experience, and supports excellent security and privacy.

- This last point brings up the very vital second initiative in this bill: funding the National Institute of Standards and Technology (NIST) to lead development of a framework of standards and operating rules to make sure these services are built in a way that sets a high bar for security and privacy. The bill recognizes from the start that any new digital identity systems, if crafted poorly, could create privacy and security concerns – and doesn't shy away from this issue. Instead, the bill tackles this head on. First by directing NIST to create a framework that engineers strong security and privacy protections in from the start, and second, by requiring that any new government systems follow this framework. There's nobody in government or the private sector with better expertise to do this than NIST. It's also worth noting on the privacy side that nothing in this bill envisions having government share data on Americans. The role of government is limited to validating – at an individual's request – that data submitted matches what a particular agency has in its authoritative identity systems. That approach significantly mitigates potential security and privacy risks with having government play a role here.

- Third, the bill would set up a new grant program to provide funding to states to help them implement this architecture and framework in state DMVs – accelerating their transition to being digital identity providers through new mobile Driver's License (mDL) apps and other digital identity solutions. All grant dollars would be tied to a state's adherence to the NIST framework, ensuring 1) that all states implement solutions that set a high bar for security and privacy, and 2) that all states implement solutions that are interoperable, ensuring that the country can get the full economic benefit of this investment. Notably, states would be required to allocate 10% of grant dollars to help people who may not be able to easily get an ID. One downside of the increased security requirements of the REAL ID Act has been that many Americans cannot easily get a driver's license, because they cannot produce or access the multiple documents needed to prove who they are.

  This particularly impacts the elderly, the poor, as well as survivors of domestic violence. New funding will allow states to better assist the most vulnerable in getting both physical and digital credentials and ensure that any investment in new identity infrastructure can benefit all Americans.
- Finally, the bill would address longstanding concerns about the overuse of the Social Security Number (SSN) as an identifier by directing the Government Accountability Office (GAO) to analyze what laws and regulations require industry or government to collect SSNs, as well as whether they are all still relevant and needed, or could be addressed through something other than the SSN.

Together, these four initiatives will create a comprehensive approach to digital identity that will prevent costly cybercrime, give businesses and consumers new confidence, improve inclusion, and foster growth and innovation across our economy. Notably, it's also an approach that does not rely on government to provide the entire solution – only those elements to which it is uniquely suited. Given all the problems we've seen in digital identity over the past year, the time for action is now – we urge Congress to pass the bill immediately.

In addition, the Coalition believes that the pending infrastructure package currently being negotiated being Congress and the White House should include funding for the state grants envisioned in the Improving Digital Identity Act. Any investment in broadband that does not also invest in a proper "identity layer" to enable Americans to use that broadband for secure and trusted transactions will fall short of its goal. A $2 billion investment can deliver a digital mobile Driver's License (mDL) to everyone in America who wants one, and create robust digital identity infrastructure that will deliver improved security, privacy, and economic growth.

If that cost seems high, consider that earlier this year, Congress approved an identical number solely to address concerns about state unemployment insurance systems tied to identity fraud prevention and benefit processing. We believe the same amount of money directed to new digital identity infrastructure in the states would be sufficient to address the majority of digital identity challenges tied to state ID systems.

The benefits of investing in digital identity go beyond stopping cybercrime and identity fraud – the economic benefits are notable. U.S. GDP could grow an extra 4% by 2030 with investments in robust digital identity infrastructure, according to a 2019 study by McKinsey.[7] And the Federal government would save billions annually by offering more online services; a 2013 government study estimated that digital identity infrastructure could save the IRS alone more than $300M each year while also enabling the IRS to deliver more trusted, high-assurance services to taxpayers through online channels.[8]

By failing to invest in digital identity infrastructure, the U.S. is leaving money on the table, while continuing to enable easy attack vectors for cybercriminals to prey on Americans.

It's worth noting that the U.S. is an outlier when compared to our peers: the UK, Europe, Australia and Canada all have significant digital identity initiatives underway, backed by the highest levels of government and significant budgets. If America does not follow, our failure to invest here will soon become an issue of economic competitiveness.

The Role of Artificial Intelligence and Machine Learning

Given that this hearing is taking place in the AI Taskforce, it seems important to talk about the role of artificial intelligence and machine learning in identity

---

[7] https://www.mckinsey.com/~/media/McKinsey/Business%20Functions/McKinsey%20Digital /Our%20Insights/Digital%20identification%20A%20key%20to%20inclusive%20growth/M GI-Digital-identification-Report.pdf.
[8] https://www.nist.gov/system/files/documents/2017/05/09/report13-2.pdf.

verification systems – looking both at the benefits AI is offering today and will offer in the future, as well as some of the potential risks that go with it.

Earlier, I framed challenges around digital identity in two buckets: those focused on identity proofing, typically at account creation – and those in authentication, used to log in to an account after it has been created.

On the ID Proofing side, there are two primary use cases where AI and ML play a role:

- The first is in remote ID proofing tools that ask a consumer to take a photo of their ID (such as a driver's license), as well as a selfie picture. In many of these products, AI/ML is used to help validate whether an ID document is real or counterfeit, as well as whether the selfie matches the photo on the ID. The role of AI/ML in these products is generally one where they "study" different documents and "learn" over time how to better tell a real driver's license or passport from a fake. In addition, AI/ML is also often used in the "facial comparison" aspect of the product. Here, we are starting to see some firms address concerns about the accuracy and consistency of some weaker face matching algorithms by shifting to algorithms based on 3D models of faces, rather than traditional 2D photos.

It is worth noting that Congress recognized the importance of these solutions in financial services in 2018 when it passed the Economic Growth, Regulatory Relief, and Consumer Protection Act. Section 213 of that bill was called the Making Online Banking Initiation Legal and Easy (MOBILE) Act, and it preempted some state laws that prevented banks from scanning a driver's license to support mobile applications for new accounts.

Today, the types of solutions detailed in the MOBILE Act are widely used – but not all of them use AI or ML, and performance of the products is inconsistent between vendors. Here it is worth noting that the FIDO Alliance has launched a new initiative to test and certify these solutions. Building on FIDO's success in developing testing and certification programs for authentication products, FIDO has now expanded its focus to identity proofing. While the certification program has not yet launched, FIDO has announced plans to establish performance criteria for these products, in partnership with a number of independent testing labs to measure whether products meet these performance criteria.

To the extent that there is a concern that that AI or ML technology used in some of these products might not measure up, this new testing and certification program will be a major asset. Many vendors are saying "trust us, our products work" – this program will verify that they actually do. I will note to the Committee that I am an advisor on this project – outside of the "hat" I wear with the Better Identity Coalition – and would be happy to talk about it further if there is interest.

- Second, AI and ML is used to deliver more accurate data-centric approaches to ID proofing. Here, vendors in the space look at lots of different signals and data sources, and use AI and ML to help predict over whether an applicant might be fraudulent or not – analyzing data and signals with algorithms that are constantly evolving and improving thanks to AI and ML, and that help companies root out fraud, including synthetic identity fraud, and make more accurate decisions.

Signals and data sources may include what can be inferred about a device being used to apply for an account, or the way a user interacts with that device as they enter their information digitally. Examining a wider set of signals and data sources provides a multi-dimensional view of identity for enriched verification, and simultaneously allows vendors and implementers to identify patterns of repeated identity fraud across government agencies and the private sector driven by sophisticated crime rings. Given that it is these crime rings that were at the heart of much of staggering losses in the past year, this is an increasingly important use of AI and ML.

While there are some concerns that algorithms used here might be biased – and that "putting the machines in charge" will lead to inequitable outcomes – most of what I have seen in the use of AI in these types of solutions, on balance, is improving equity and inclusion. For example, if a bank is looking at credit report data for identity proofing – but a consumer has a thin file, as is common for young people, immigrants, and historically marginalized groups – AI and ML can be used to look at other data sources and approve applicants at a higher rate. Likewise, if a consumer does not have a driver's license or passport – or does not have a smartphone – those "selfie match" tools I discussed earlier probably won't work. Again, these are areas where tools that leverage AI and ML are often able to help fill in the "gaps" and provide an alternative path to approval.

Overall, many of our members in the financial services space report that without AI/ML and risk-based models it would be difficult to perform thorough risk-based identity validation at scale.

On the Authentication side, AI and ML also play an important role as part of analytics solutions that look at dozens of different data points and signals about how an individual is 1) trying to authenticate or 2) interacting with a device or application after initial authentication.

Here, we are seeing firms in financial services and other sectors use tools that look at data such as behavior, location, typing pattern, access requests (trying to get to something they should not have access to), etc. The tools then study all these elements and then use AI to make a prediction as to whether anything seems "off" or shows a sign of account or device compromise.

By pairing more traditional authentication such as that using the FIDO standards with analytics solutions that use AI/ML to "score" in real time the likelihood that an account remains in the hands of its rightful owner, we are closer than ever to eliminating reliance on passwords.

The emergence of reliable authentication analytics tools is contributing to the rise of a new model for authentication called "continuous, risk-based authentication." Here you pair a traditional authentication factor like a password or MFA with analytics tools that analyze different signals. Some might automatically remediate a sign of fraud by refusing authentication, in other cases it might trigger a signal that is then used to ask a user for additional factors of authentication. To be clear, not all of these tools use AI and ML, but many do.

As major banks and cloud providers see tens or hundreds of millions of fraudulent attacks each day on their login systems, AI and ML have emerged as essential tools to detect and block them.

Having offered this brief primer on how AI and ML are used in identity proofing an authentication, I'd like to offer the Task Force a few thoughts on how policymakers should think about these technologies going forward.

1. First, the points I just detailed should make clear that AI and ML technologies are an increasingly important tool in identity – particularly given the ongoing battle we are in against cybercriminals. These criminals are doubling or in some cases quintupling down on identity-centric attacks, putting the security and privacy of people's data and money at risk. The good guys need every tool in the toolbox.

On that point, criminals themselves are starting to develop their own AI and ML tools to support cyber-attacks. This is slightly terrifying but should not be surprising; the same technology innovations that can be used to protect us will also be exploited by adversaries to try to attack us. We're seeing this in the early stages with criminals using bots for automated password spray and credential stuffing attacks. Attackers are always innovating, and we should be preparing for them to be using AI against us in new and innovative ways.
2. Second, To the point that there are policy concerns about the use of AI and ML, the answer is not to ban their use but rather to identify the specific concerns and work to address them. Because a blanket ban will almost certainly play into the hands of criminals and put consumers and businesses at great risk.
3. Third, an important part of issues surrounding AI and ML used in identity verification is the fact that many of the technologies are opaque: despite the efficiency of many algorithms, it still difficult to explain their decisions to most people. These issues can be greatly mitigated by independent certification and testing programs such as the one for remote ID proofing tools that I mentioned earlier that FIDO Alliance is developing – creating a way to independently validate the claims made by vendors and also determine whether there are any specific quirks or biases in a product or algorithm that may need to be addressed. In addition, NIST has done some great work to help vendors and implementers address potential bias concerns in its recent draft Special Publication 1270, *"A Proposal for Identifying and Managing Bias in Artificial Intelligence."*
4. Fourth, it is important that policymakers do not lose sight of the ways AI and ML can help with inclusion and equity. As I mentioned earlier, financial services firm are already starting to use AI to enable new approaches to identity proofing that can help bring more services to the "credit invisible" – such as more easily auto-approving more people for loans – relative to legacy tools that don't use AI.
5. Finally, I would state that the single best way to address concerns with regard to bias in AI and ML being used in identity proofing tools is to pass the Improving Digital Identity Act. In that every product using AI and ML to try to determine identity is trying to "guess" what only the government really knows. And there is no better way to address concerns about these probabilistic systems run amuck than to enable new deterministic systems that rely on the actual source of identity in

government. As I have stated throughout my testimony, we're not going to truly solve identity proofing without the kinds of identity attribute validation services that the bill calls for.

In closing, while the current state of digital identity poses some challenges, Chairman Foster and his colleagues have put before Congress a proposal that will address these challenges in a complete and holistic fashion. The time to act on it is now.

I am grateful for the Committee's invitation to offer recommendations on how government can improve the identity ecosystem and look forward to your questions.

Mobile Driver's Licenses, Backgrounder and Written Testimony, House Financial Services Committee, Hearing on Verifying Identity while Preserving Privacy in the Digital Age

Abstract

Consumers view putting their ID Card or Driver's License on their mobile device as the last step toward the freedom of not carrying a wallet. The technology to do this exists today. Implementing Mobile Driver's License to meet the goals of privacy, equity, and freedom in American Society while ensuring higher security for American identities is the challenge. The Trust Frameworks for meeting these challenges also exist. Coordination and enforcement of business, legal, and technology can help meet American values in an Identity Ecosystem.

July 16, 2021,
A. David Kelts
david@kelts.org ·
https://www.linkedin.com/in/dkelts/@DavidKelts

Honorable Chair and Committee Members,
I am David Kelts from Arlington, Massachusetts, representing myself in support of forming a Mobile Driver's License ecosystem that reinforces the American values of privacy, equity, and freedom while spurring innovation and improvement.

I am the Director of Product Development for Mobile ID at GET Group North America, and a 5-year member of ISO/IEC JTC1/SC17/WG10 that wrote the 18013-5 mDL Standard. I lead the Evangelism Task Force within Working Group 10, and I was a lead author of the Privacy Annex of 18013-5. I am also a committee member and lead contributor to the Secure Technology Alliance's Identity Council, participating in mDL education efforts. The views I present today are my own proposals for your consideration.

I have prepared a Mobile Driver's License backgrounder in the attached pages. I will summarize the recommendations therein in this written testimony.

A Mobile Driver's License is a digitally signed document placed onto the mDL Holder's mobile phone for them to control. Government Issuers around the globe are the signers. When the user consents to share, individual data elements from their ID can be transmitted to a Reader device (Verifier). This is an improvement over physical cards where all data is visible on the front and decodable from the barcode. ISO 18013-5 is a standard for in-person, attended ID transactions, complementing existing online standards. The mDL Standard is designed to fit next to online identity standards such as Open ID Connect and user authentication standards such as from The Fido Alliance.

Empowering Americans with a mobile identity document carries challenges and must meet the values and goals of Americans. Protecting identity information, giving greater control and flexibility to the rightful holder of the identity, and supporting accuracy of operations come with the goals of inclusivity and access for all Americans.

There are challenges to getting a Mobile Driver's License ecosystem started. Government identity card Issuers must take the first move since they are the signatories to the accuracy and provenance of mDL Data. Support for their digital transformation that meets American goals can kickstart this digital identity transformation and help ensure that privacy and inclusiveness is achieved. Their decision thus far to embark on digital transformation and issue mDLs has been largely driven by desire to be technical leaders or through legislative mandate. The mechanisms to fund this transformation have not been easy to find, and Consumer Pays models are largely being chosen. It is worth funding this digital transformation.

Challenges exist on the Verifier side as well. Businesses and Government Agencies that accept ID and Driver's Licenses will wait for a large number of mDL holders before investing in technology for Contactless ID that can help protect their employees' health and safety. Restaurants, for example, have moved to contactless menus out of necessary, but still must check ID manually by handling another person's ID card. Spurring innovation and the deployment of systems that accept mDL can bring Contactless ID transactions into reality. The technology is functional. Priming the pump of the business model to spur innovation would be helpful.

Identity, and the Mobile Driver's License Ecosystem, operates as a sum of many parts. The glue which holds together shared goals and values of such an ecosystem is a Trust Framework. Trust Frameworks define the business, legal, and technical "rules of the road" for an identity ecosystem. This framework is achieved in other regions by government-led initiatives, privately operated frameworks, or public-private partnership. To meet the goals and values of Americans, I recommend initiating a public-private partnership chartered to determine requirements based on our values and to enforce those requirements.

Federal Agencies have an opportunity to lead a digital transformation by accepting mDL in manners that help protect the health and safety of their Agents and Americans. The Transportation Security Administration, fueled in part by the exposure of TSA Agents to corona virus, has led this kind of transformation toward accepting mDLs by participating in the creation of the standard and industry efforts to educate and initiate deployment. Funding Federal Agencies toward this deployment will save lives and reinforce values.

The Department of Homeland Security has invested in the development of technologies for online identity. Similar initiatives to spur innovation, new development, and the deployment of privacy-enhancing, accessible technologies for accepting mDL can complement existing efforts by adding the in-person transactions all of us perform with identity documents.

Industry Efforts, such as those by the Secure Technology Alliance, Better Identity Coalition, Kantara Initiative, Future Identity Council, and others welcome the continued and expanded investment by the Federal Government and Federal Agencies. There is expertise to be shared in bringing effective digital identity into reality in a way that reinforces our values.

Thank you,

Backgrounder: What is Mobile Driver's License (mDL)?

A Mobile Driver's License is a digitally signed document placed onto the mDL Holder's mobile phone for them to control. Government Issuers around the globe are the signers. When the user consents to share, individual data elements from their ID can be transmitted to a Reader device (Verifier). This is an improvement over physical cards where all data is visible on the front and decodable from the barcode. ISO 18013-5 is a standard for in-person, attended ID transactions, complementing existing online standards.

Electronic Images of ID Cards Are Insecure and Easy to Spoof

Most people immediately think that you show your mDL to a verifier. Photo editing tools and spoof applications make this impossible to trust. Imagine the fraud if we were showing Credit Card numbers on phone screens as payment. After unlocking the mDL app, the mDL Holder taps their phone or shows a QR code to a Reader. That action means the mDL Holder wants to share.

Initially, they share a connection token.

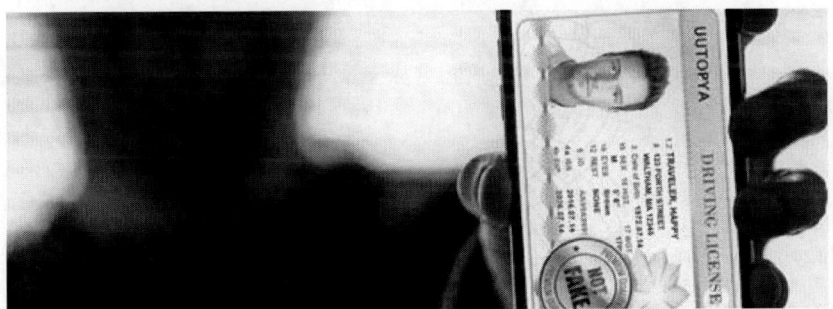

Figure 1. Showing a phone screen is simple to spoof. Tap or Scan for cryptographic proof of ID and encrypted data sharing.

Cryptographic Proof of ID Data – Token to Share

The initial token does not contain any identifying information about the mDL Holder. Its purely a token setting up a transfer, which is the same methodology used for electronic tap payments. The token is exchanged for data by the Reader through a Web API (server retrieval) or directly from the mDL (device retrieval). Either model ensures encrypted transfer of data and resists eavesdropping or replay.

Control over Data Sharing and Device; Collection Limitation and Business Need to Store

The phone never leaves the mDL Holder's hand and they have granular consent over the data they share. The Reader asks just for the data they require, and gets cryptographic proof that the subset of mDL Data is intact, unaltered, and came directly from the Issuer. This is how Contactless ID transactions can be accomplished. Since accurate, fresh data is available at each transaction, it is no longer architecturally required for Verifiers to store customer data. Data that is not stored does not expose a business to liability of leaks.

The demand for Contactless payment has grown significantly during the past 18-months, while Contactless ID verification has not been possible. Protecting the health and safety of the American public, business employees, and Federal Agents such as TSA is critical.

Figure 2. Contactless ID transactions with ISO 18013-5.

Multiple Interaction Modes

ISO 18013-5 is a data transmission protocol for trusted data. Sharing data is always initiated by the mDL Holder and nothing ever leaves the device without mDL Holder consent. The current version of the standard supports QR code and NFC tap to initiate connection, NFC, Bluetooth, and WiFi Aware for device retrieval of mDL Data (offline when not connected to the Internet), and REST API and Open ID Connect for server-retrieval of mDL Data (when online). This is the same Open ID connect widely used for login to web sites.

This means that mDLs can support multiple different interaction modes[9] at different distances. Interaction Modes support different workflows that businesses and agencies that accept mDL can deploy for faster customer processing, more trustworthy transactions, and enhanced customer privacy. ISO 18013-5 mDL is presently designed for in-person transactions.

---

[9] https://www.securetechalliance.org/publications-the-mobile-drivers-license-mdl-and-eco system/section 2.3 defines and names the Interaction Modes of an mDL.

Security of Data in Transit When Using ISO 18013-5

The token that kicks off an mDL device-retrieval contains key material that is combined with key material from the Reader device to create a one-time encrypted transmit session. No nearby device can eavesdrop on a session because it cannot generate the same decryption keys. The public key of the Government Issuer is used to validate that the mDL Data was not altered and is official ID.

For server-retrieval, the public key of the Government Issuer is used to secure the channel to an online web service. This is equivalent to connecting to a website and seeing the lock icon in the browser. Data is never released without a token granting permission by the mDL Holder or without transaction-time identity verification and consent from Open ID Connect (that is widely used across login systems).

In both models, unlinkable identifiers and rotating public keys can be used to ensure some level of anonymity of the consumer participating in the transaction. Both models were created from the beginning using Privacy By Design principles. It is, on the other hand, possible in either device-retrieval or server-retrieval models to make mistakes or intentionally violate privacy principles. The technology for privacy must always be paired with the business models and legal protection to meet shared goals.

A Truly International Standard

Members of the ISO Working Group over the last 5 years included hundreds of participants from over 50 companies representing countries from every inhabited continent. Meetings were held in Africa, Asia, Australia, Europe, and North America to ensure accessibility to meetings and content. mDL Interoperability Tests have been held in Japan, Brisbane, and Omaha, NE. mDL pilot programs and contracts have been implemented in Sweden, Kosovo, New South Wales, Queensland, Ecuador, Indonesia, and multiple US States[10]. mDL Standard development was contributed to by AAMVA, eReg, Austroads, and the Motor Vehicle Associations of each continent. AAMVA has published guidelines[11] for North American issuers that mandate the use of ISO 18013-5 mDL.

---

[10] https://www.mdlconnection.com/implementation-tracker-map/ shows updated mDL progress.
[11] https://www.aamva.org/mDL-Resources/.

Privacy Assessments Performed

Assessments of mDL Technology and the potential for a positive impact on privacy have been published. These are exceptionally well-researched, well-written publications fairly representing the concerns of Americans and technologists world-wide. They express concerns, positives, and shortcomings.

- *Annex E: Privacy & Security Recommendations*, ISO/IEC FDIS 18013-5:2021 (E)[12]
- ACLU: *Identity Crisis* What Digital Driver's License Could Mean for Privacy, Equity, and Freedom[13]
- Kantara Initiative, *Privacy & Identity Protection in mDL*[14]
- Google Security Blog: *Privacy Preserving Features in the Mobile Driver's License*[15]

The universal recommendation is that mDL holds promise with a warning. If done well, mDL can improve our privacy and identity security. To ensure that mDL is, in fact done well, will take a coordinated Business, Legal, and Technology effort such as in-place in other parts of the world (see Regional Fit below).

References – What Has Been Written About mDL?

One of the first and most comprehensive white papers on the mDL is *The Mobile Driver's License (mDL) and Ecosystem*[16], from the Secure Technology Alliance. It is accompanied by an Executive Summary and a series of informative webinars[17] on mDL. Privacy, Trust, Business Model, and an Operating Framework for trust are key topics and concepts explained in this series.

The Mobile Driver's License (mDL) and Ecosystem accurately describes advantages of mDL, its flexible use, and the challenges that the mDL ecosystem, or any identity ecosystem, will face as it gets started with nascent

---

[12] https://isotc.iso.org/livelink/livelink?func=ll&objId=21927996&objAction=Open, Annex E.
[13] https://www.aclu.org/report/identity-crisis-what-digital-drivers-licenses-could-mean-privacy-equity-and-freedom.
[14] https://docs.kantarainitiative.org/PImDL-V1-Final.html.
[15] https://security.googleblog.com/2020/10/privacy-preserving-features-in-mobile.html.
[16] https://www.securetechalliance.org/publications-the-mobile-drivers-license-mdl-and-ecosystem/.
[17] https://www.securetechalliance.org/the-mobile-drivers-license-and-ecosystem-webinar-series/.

technology trying to meet the needs of many. Section 6 of the white paper on *Challenges to a Robust mDL Ecosystem* is the rallying call around which Secure Technology Alliance members will collaborate to solve problems for years to come.

mDL Programs are in various states of development in the United States. The most accurate map of the present-day advancement of mDL Technology is available from mDL-Connection.com[18]. It is evident that the pace of these developments is quickening. Cross-state testing is beginning to happen, and use cases are being deployed in banking, retail, age-based purchase, restricted goods purchase, car-rental, transportation, and law enforcement. All are presently in-person with eventual online use case extensions.

How Did mDL Create an Ecosystem?

Two Participants in a Transaction Plus the Signatory
In every mDL transaction, there is the mDL Holder who consents to share a subset of their identity information with a Verifier to receive a service or good for which confirmation of government-issued identity attributes is required. That Government Issuer, passively, is the third participant in the transaction. This naturally forms an Ecosystem.

ISO 18013-5 mDL allows that third participant to be entirely passive – they can make known the public key that confirms their signature on the mDL Data and their position as an authoritative identity proofer in the eyes of the Verifier (who chooses the public keys that they trust and will accept).

---

[18] https://www.mdlconnection.com/implementation-tracker-map/.

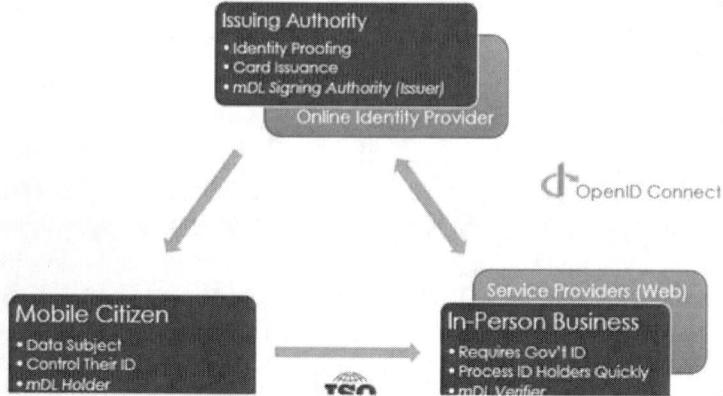

Figure 3. Participants in mDL in-person ecosystem (blue) next to the predominant online identity system (gray).

Every Issuer from the initial AAMVA Guidelines to present has stated that they wish their participation to remain passive. Tracking and surveillance will not by policy or technology be tolerated.

ISO 18013-5 mDL was designed to create an ecosystem for in-person transactions. The secondary intention was to ensure that these in-person transactions could exist beside and in harmony with identity-backed transactions in the online, web world. ISO 18013-5 can work very well next to Open ID Connect. Open ID Connect is the majority technology in use for login credential providers. Adding unattended transactions has always been envisioned as utilizing Fido Alliance user authentication – a privacy-enhancing, flexible standard for authenticating users.

Many open source and SaaS implementations of Open ID Connect are widely available and highly functional. It is expected the same will hold true for mDL implementations.

Viewpoints of "Trust" from Those Participants

In addition to the convenience of potentially not carrying their wallet, Consumers (mDL Holders) will use and trust their mDL if it makes their life easier, protects their identity better than currently, is accepted everywhere, and provides them the opportunity for Contactless ID transactions.

Verifiers are typically business with requirements to accept government-issued ID. They need the reliability of an always available system that cannot be spoofed, will protect their employees from disease transmission, and will accurately identify the person to whom they are granting the transaction.

Issuers also, from their arm's length of these transactions, need to accurately provision each mDL to the right citizen and trust the distribution mechanisms for their public keys (sometimes called PKDs). They also may need to make the technology decisions to ensure the high-availability and security of their deployment systems and the mobile applications.

When any one of these viewpoints of trust falls short, trust in the ecosystem will begin to erode. This is why kickstarting the ecosystem, ensuring its smooth and seamless operation, and providing enforcement capabilities with consumer redress actions is necessary for mDL to be trusted and used.

In blockchain or distributed ledger identity systems, there is potentially an additional entity in the ecosystem – those with the privilege to write to the ledger. This privileged group is often formed by consortium and the privileged ledger-writers are called Stewards. Other models exist.

Additional Objectives of mDL in an Ecosystem

mDL Usage by Americans is predicated on fulfilling certain privacy, security, and convenience goals. mDL Holders can be given the opportunity to choose their solution that fits these values (as in the model chosen by the State of Florida[19,20]), and Issuers can choose to provide these values in the applications they select for their residents. ISO 18013-5 mDL provides the opportunity to achieve these goals.

---

[19] https://www.flhsmv.gov/floridasmartid/.
[20] https://www.wtsp.com/article/news/regional/florida/florida-drivers-license/67-ff420646-1c55-40c7-99cd-55acb3c0e296.

Privacy	Security	Convenience
• Full control of your ID document • Share only what you consent • Protect your Health	• Encryption that only you unlock • Secure private transmission with a tap or scan	• Runs on your existing phone • Accepted Everywhere around the Globe • NOT Proprietary

Regional Values

Inclusivity – Equal Access to All – is a clear objective of identity systems to re-enfranchise those who may be missing documentation of their birth and name. The technology itself must operate equitably. State Government Issuers – DMVs – operate with identity proofing guidelines that allow the vast majority access. In many municipalities, City IDs have attempted to fill any gaps in inclusiveness. All can be targets for mDL given that the businesses and agencies accepting mDL decide from which Issuers they will accept mobile identities.

In the United States, privacy, freedom, and inclusiveness are national values with the additional technological goals of interoperability, ease of use, and accuracy of identification.

Regional Fit

For use of an mDL to meet the objectives of any region around the world, it must operate within a Trust Framework that defines the Business, Legal, and Technical "rules of the road" for identity operations. Such frameworks can be privately operated, as in the example of a consortium like Sovrin[21], government operated, as in the example of TDIF[22] from the Australian Digital Transformation Agency, or a public-private partnership such as DIACC Pan-Canadian Trust Framework[23] in Canada. In addition, technology companies with the means to implement an end-to-end solution could also privately operate a trust framework for mDL or online identities.

---

[21] https://sovrin.org/library/sovrin-governance-framework/.
[22] https://www.dta.gov.au/our-projects/digital-identity/trusted-digital-identity-framework.
[23] https://diacc.ca/trust-framework/.

Why Hasn't mDL Happened Already?

Demand Is Growing, the Catalyst Is Missing

To turn the wheels of this nascent mDL Ecosystem, typically the Government Issuer must be the first to act. The impetus and business rationale for action of a State Agency is not always clear. Standing out as a technology leader and achieving the public good are currently the determining or driving factors in a decision to pursue mDL.

In Utah[24], the Driver's License Division[25] has taken first action upon legislative mandate and had the foresight to include business partners in the evaluation of a public contract award process. Businesses such as Utah Consumer Credit Union[26] have jumped to the forefront to accept mDLs before they were widely issued and have seen a boost in their membership due to technology leadership.

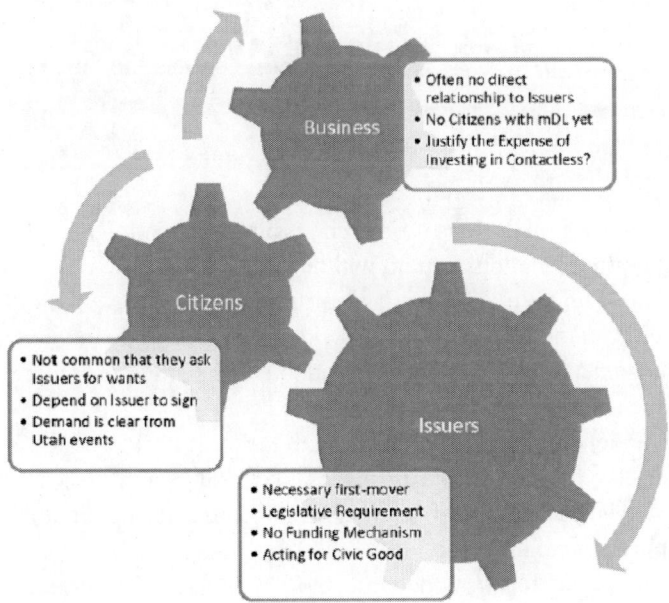

---

[24] Please note that the author's employer is affiliated with each entity used in this example of ecosystem startup. The author has worked directly on these products and project.
[25] https://publicsafety.utah.gov/2021/04/20/new-mobile-driver-license-to-offer-utahns-enhanced-privacy/.
[26] https://www.cutimes.com/2021/06/24/utah-community-cu-to-test-mobile-drivers-licenses/.

No Uniform Business Model

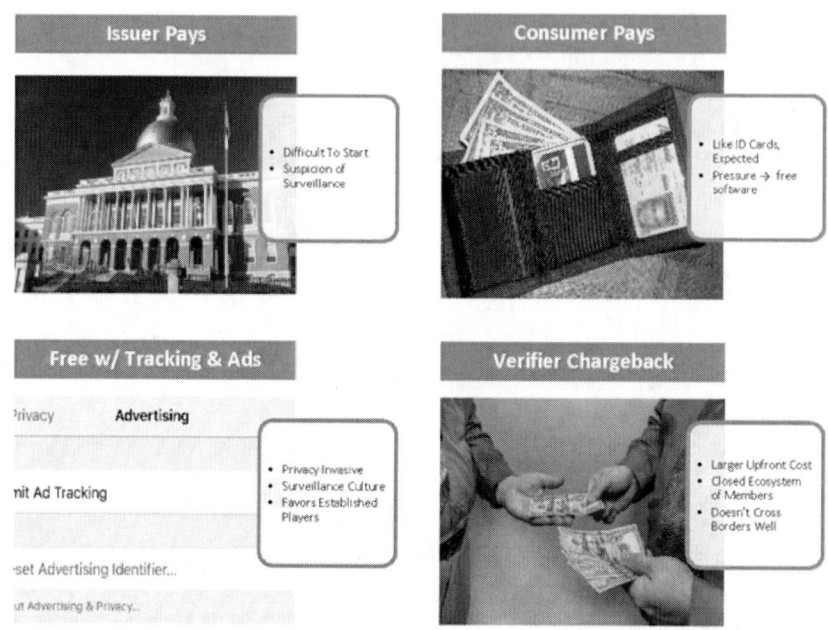

ISO 18013-5 mDL does not specify a business model, it is a technology interchange specification. Issuers without funding that want to act on behalf of their citizens face a difficult choice to move first. In the USA, the Consumer-Pays model fits with how residents currently pay for physical cards, so the Consumer Pays model has been adopted when high-technology vendors provide the solution.

The model of Issuers developing mDL technology (therefore Issuer Pays) is also in use, in the US and in places like New South Wales, with those solutions now needing to retrofit an mDL standard and find funding to expand beyond purely local usage.

Verifier Chargeback models are most effective when the ecosystem is closed-loop, membership led, or operated by a single entity or consortium. This allows for an accounting system that funnels money in a highly appropriate way – from those whose risk is reduced, and processes are improved (Verifiers) back to those who did the work to proof the individual identities (Issuers). Verifier Chargeback is difficult to kick-start because often the entire system must be in place before money starts flowing. Governance in these systems includes accounting services as well as Trust Framework enforcement.

Free With *Tracking and Ads* is a business model widely in use across the Internet today. If the software is free, you the User are likely the product. This model is largely why today's hearing exists. Mixing mDL with this business model is likely to feel extremely creepy to Americans and deter usage.

What Happens without a Catalyst or Business Model?

Lacking the catalyst or precipitant to kick-start any of these business models or the mDL Ecosystem, it is highly likely that a large player with deep pockets will step in to impose their business model on the mDL Ecosystem.

The *Verifier-Chargeback* model is one option when pockets are deep enough that the up-front development costs could be entirely R&D funded. The owner of the mDL Ecosystem in this model would own the chargeback mechanisms at a percentage analogous to those of software application distribution mechanisms (App Stores). Even if that technology giant only provided half of the mDL devices in the Ecosystem, the price pressure on the other half of smartphone applications would be driven to zero. The Consumer Pays model would be eradicated. The expectation of free software could drive ad or privacy-invasive funding alternatives. Privacy, in general, for all identity transactions flowing through one system could then become the responsibility of one tech giant to carry out.

Another potential move toward a *Free With Tracking and Ads* business model could be precipitated by other technology giants. To date, data on identity-backed business transactions with visual inspection of physical cards is not consolidated or correlated. It is possible with systems that scan PDF417[27] barcodes.

None of the above testimony is other than informed speculation about the possibilities of the development of the mDL Ecosystem. What is clear is that the business model and legal framework for an mDL Ecosystem must reflect the values of the American people and the ecosystem must remain open to many participants to provide and extract value – a free market. The physical ID market has many players, starting with innovators and, as with many mature markets, gravitating toward consolidation, consistency, or stagnation. Technology improvements have made the manufacture of fake IDs easier. Cryptography improvements will be the moving target of the mDL Ecosystem to stay ahead of forgeries.

---

[27] https://www.aamva.org/DL-ID-Card-Design-Standard/ contains PDF417 data formatting.

What Protections Are Necessary?

Security Standards to Avoid a Privacy Problem
Any Trust Framework would contain Business, Legal, and Technical rules by which all participants abide. Participants must abide by these rules and requirements to continue operation. Enforcement is both voluntary, collective, and backed by rules of recourse.

ISO 18013-5 mDL provides security mechanisms for data in-transit, but the secure storage of data is not specified. The security of mDL Data when stored on mobile phone, in cloud repositories, or even in aged, single-location, on-premise data centers is not part of a data transmission standard. Minimum acceptable standards for data at rest must be designated and measurable. Google has advanced this concept on Android with its Identity Credential API[28,29]. Security audits and compliance certifications should be made available to all participants in the ecosystem by all providers.

Privacy Is a Collective Responsibility
Identity protection and the resulting privacy is always an Ecosystem responsibility shared among all participants. A failure in security by any one participant can compromise the privacy of many. For this reason, enforcement must be available and channels to resolve and remedy dispute must exist. The current environment for binding together mDL implementations in the US may be State laws.

In my many discussions with State Issuers, every single one wants to distance themselves from person-to-verifier transactions. The technology for unlinkable transactions is available and the will exists.

Where Does the Consumer Turn for Protection?
Enforcement of Consumer Protection of Privacy has developed into the responsibility of the Federal Trade Commission. mDL is an evolution of present day card-based in-person transactions, and similar enforcement may be applicable when mDL transactions begin to happen during 2021 – 2022.

The question of consumer protection is not the expertise of the author, but a concern highlighted in order for it to be addressed in appropriate channels.

---

[28] https://developer.android.com/reference/android/security/identity/IdentityCredentialStore.
[29] https://www.xda-developers.com/google-android-digital-drivers-license/.

Considerations for Federal Action

Action to organize the Trust Framework, and the enforcement of it within the United States is recommended. It should take a form suitably organized and agile for the technology world of 2021+ so that it is adaptable to change and always carries out the principles and vision of Americans. NIST previously was chartered with organizing and running an Identity Ecosystem Steering Group (IDESG[30]) responsible for defining how identity could work in the US. The remnants of the IDESG and charter are now part of Kantara Initiative. Technology has evolved sufficiently that many of the visions of the 2000's and 2010's, including those piloted in many NSTIC[31] Grants, have become feasible and usable. This sort of public-private partnership toward shared common goals is still viable in the US.

The Secure Technology Alliance has many members in the Verifier space. STA is currently responding to the active *DHS/TSA Request For Information* with a set of considerations for DHS and Federal Agencies to assist with the formation of the mDL Ecosystem in a way that reflects American values and creates a playing field for innovation and growth. The following is an excerpt used with permission.

> STA commends DHS, and its component TSA, for active participation in early efforts by STA to start to overcome the challenges [outlined in Section 6 of The Mobile Driver's License (mDL) Ecosystem (ed.)].
> STA now recommends:
>
> a) Strengthening DHS engagement in the concepts and efforts to kickstart the ecosystem. STA welcomes and encourages DHS participation at STA and at the other industry groups working toward the realization of a secure mDL Ecosystem
> b) Defining the security, provisioning, and privacy requirements that attach meaning to the "Real ID" flag defined in the AAMVA Guidelines since RealID is central to the acceptance of mDL for Federal Use Cases
> c) Encouraging all federal agencies and interagency bodies to participate in overcoming these challenges and realizing the ecosystem

---

[30] https://idesg.edufoundation.kantarainitiative.org/ IDESG now part of Kantara Initiative.
[31] https://en.wikipedia.org/wiki/National_Strategy_for_Trusted_Identities_in_Cyberspace.

d) Using STA Use Case Development resources (published along with the white paper) to capture and publish business processes and interactions where federal agencies rely upon driver's licenses or where a trusted digital ID credential could:
- Reduce risk and control costs
- Enhance quality of life, service, and user experience
- Promote the growing interest in touch-free interaction
- Reduce fraud that harms the privacy, security, or identity of our countrymen

e) Utilizing available funding, such as Silicon Valley Innovation Program, to roll out the acceptance of mDL for Federal Use cases. This program has been successful at pursuing architectural goals, and can now be used to encourage adoption of Contactless ID at scale in order to protect the health of our nation and improve security

f) Lobbying for the nationwide legislation and funding that will encourage States to issue, businesses to accept, and citizens to have contactless options available to them

g) Empowering and educating Federal Agencies with the authority to enforce privacy standards and requirements across mDL usage in the ecosystem within the USA

Since the publication of the STA White Paper, demand for Contactless ID transactions has grown proportional to the growth in usage of Contactless Payment. The potential health benefits are clear in a post-covid world, and the protection of TSA Agents, Federal Employees, and the general public are critical to the operation and security of our country. STA encourages DHS to utilize whatever resources are available to assist a transition to a Contactless ID society.

Relying Party interest in accepting mDL as official government ID is blossoming inside STA and in the ecosystem at large. These driving forces of ecosystem momentum and healthier contactless ID are fueling interest and development.

Outside of the STA White Paper, members experiences in the implementation of state and major urban center identity programs prove that momentum is growing rapidly. They also seem to reiterate and compound the Least Common Denominator (LCD) problem described in STA White Paper section 6.1. The compounding of this LCD problem is, in practice in the field in jurisdictions that are rolling out mDL, slowing the number of locations where mDL will be accepted Day One and opening the door to competing standards not geared toward in-person usage. There are three major points where LCD is happening:

1. NFC that is widely used at point of sale and point of service is not available for mDL communications on all major phone operating systems, which results in hesitancy of Relying Parties to adopt or to bias their acceptance mDL to just the Android platform.
2. Vendor implementations that include a single Interaction Mode (see section 2 of STA White Paper that names these Interaction Modes) simply to achieve a rubberstamp of conformity are limiting the choices of relying parties in how they will accept mDL. In fact, some implementations have mutually exclusive technologies for mDL interaction, leaving Relying Parties considering waiting before they accept mDL. Wait and see approaches can hurt mDL ecosystem momentum.
3. Visual approaches that short-circuit cryptographic proof of identity are being rolled out in States because the ecosystem is not developed, and Federal Agencies (as well as other relying parties) are not yet equipped to accept mDL transmission and cryptography. Since there is no way to secure the screen renderings of mobile devices (the secure elements do not protect screen memory), visual implementations are injecting uncertainty into concept of mDL and exposing the potential for this mDL marketplace to blow up before it gains full momentum.

STA encourages DHS participation to alleviate these developing shortcomings in the ecosystem, fund the transition to cryptographic proof of identity at all agency points of service, promote what is known to be acceptably secure and fraud-resistant solutions, and seed the development of relying party technology to accept mDL. Innovation Programs within DHS could be tuned to develop acceptance of mDL and not just to solve online identity or espouse particular architectures.

Major considerations for achieving public or industry acceptance are:

- The security and identity assurance level of the mDL provisioning process (Section 5.2)

- The security of the smart device that hosts the mDL credential and its platform
- Verifier trust in the credential across states, countries, and other jurisdictions (Section 5)
- Verifier trust that the credential is in possession of the proper, intended Holder (Section 5)
- Enforcement of privacy protection for mDL Holders (Section 5.3) across all Interaction Modes
- Liability and safety considerations for Verifiers and mDL Holders
- Incentives of any form, including tax incentives such as those spurring electric vehicle markets, that allow Verifiers to adopt as pioneers in the mDL Ecosystem. This speeds up the transition to Contactless ID that will protect security and health of citizens.

Other considerations include:

- Phasing of feature roll-out and avoiding the risk of least common denominator solutions
- Eradicating solutions with visual presentation or unsigned, unprotected barcode data
- Verifier understanding of state and global or regional policies for proofing and issuance
- Testing, education, and training for Issuers, Holders, and Verifiers
- mDL Holder signing functionality for use cases where "signing with your ID" is warranted
- Adoption of standardized user authentication for assisted or unattended use cases

The text box above is quoted with permission from The Secure Technology Alliances' response to DHS/TSA active Request for Information on Mobile Driver's Licenses.

House Financial Services AI Task Force, I Am Who I Say I Am: Verifying Identity While Preserving Privacy in the Digital Age, July 16th 2021, Dr Louise Maynard-Atem, Women in Identity

Good afternoon and thank you Chairman Foster, Ranking Member Gonzales and the other members of the task force for the opportunity to testify today.

My name is Louise Maynard-Atem and I'm the research lead for the non-profit organisation Women in Identity; an organisation whose mission is to ensure that digital identity solutions are designed with the diverse communities that they serve in mind. We are a volunteer-led and member-focused organisation, and all work full-time in the digital identity sector. Women in Identity is entirely independent and not acting in the interests of any one organisation or individual. Instead, our volunteers and members are united by the belief that we need to make identity systems that work for everyone, ensure that they are inclusive for all and free from bias. Today I will be representing the views of Women in Identity, but it is also pertinent to the topic of today's hearing to mention my full-time role. I lead the data insights function at GBG, an identity and fraud organisation whose mission is to drive trust and confidence in digital transactions through the provision of identity proofing services.

The specific topic I would like to focus on today is that of inclusion and bias. The need for improved digital identity systems and infrastructure has been a pressing requirement for many years, as more businesses have moved their operations online. The pandemic has accelerated that shift online, and increased the focus on the need for digital identity infrastructure over the last 18 months. This presents us with a unique opportunity to enable economic and societal value creation as digital identity systems are the gatekeeper to access services like online banking, e-commerce and insurance. However, we also need to recognise that the use of technology in digital identity systems has the potential to further entrench, and potentially exacerbate, the exclusionary and biased practises that persist in society today. Simply digitising what were previously analog processes and utilising flawed data would be a missed opportunity to deliver systems and services that benefit all citizens.

At Women in Identity we believe that inclusion doesn't just happen on its own. In order for identity systems to be inclusive and free from bias, the requirement for it must be mandated. There are many examples where exclusion and bias have not been explicitly mandated against within identity systems, and in many of those instances identity systems have been built which have excluded certain groups, often because of particular characteristics such as skin colour, gender, culture, socio-economic background or disabilities. Examples include:

- Up to a third of adults (women and the elderly were particularly affected) in Kenya were excluded from healthcare and social services due to lack of a national ID card, a prerequisite for gaining access to the country's digital identity card[32]
- According to a member of the Iraqi Commission for Human Rights quoted in Kurdistan, 1.5 million Iraqis born between 2001 and 2003 and who should be voting for the first time, will not be able to do so as their names are not on the voter register and they have not received their biometric or temporary cards.[33]

According to recent population statistics for adults in the United States:

- Approx. 11% of American adults don't have government issued ID documents (which is approximately 20m people)[34]
- Approx. 18% of American adults don't use a smartphone[35]
- 5.4% of US households are unbanked (approximately 7.1m households)[36]

The lack of government issued ID, ownership of a smartphone or bank account can often be some of the building blocks used in creating a digital identity for an individual. There are many and varied reasons for the above, but it is essential that any digital identity solution is accessible to all of these groups, and does not cause them to be further excluded from the opportunities that such technology-driven solutions may become the gatekeeper for.

---

[32] https://www.theguardian.com/global-development/2021/jun/09/ugandas-id-scheme-excludes-nearly-a-third-from-healthcare-says-report.
[33] https://www.biometricupdate.com/202106/biometric-card-delays-exclude-millions-from-iraq-elections.
[34] https://www.learningforjustice.org/sites/default/files/general/Percentage%20of%20People%20Who%20Lack%20ID_0.pdf.
[35] https://newzoo.com/insights/rankings/top-countries-by-smartphone-penetration-and-users/.
[36] https://www.fdic.gov/analysis/household-survey/index.html.

In the physical world, we would never erect buildings that weren't accessible to all (features like wheelchair ramps are mandatory). We need to ensure we are mandating equivalent accessibility in the digital world.

Establishing an inclusive identity system requires an exclusion risk assessment and explicit strategies to ensure access to identification for all, with particular attention to groups that are at higher risk of exclusion, such as remote and rural residents, ethnic and linguistic minorities, people with disabilities, marginalized women and girls, and those with low technical literacy.[37] As part of the planning process, decision makers should also carefully consider the exclusion risks of formalizing or increasing identification/authentication requirements for different transactions.

What we are observing is a move towards identity trust frameworks being developed around the world, where the need for inclusion and testing for bias is being explicitly called out. To share some insight into how inclusion in digital identity is being thought about here in the UK, I wanted to discuss the UK Digital Identity and Attribute Trust Framework[38] that Women in Identity was involved in consulting on. The UK trust framework, published in alpha form in February 2021, sets out requirements to help organisations understand what 'good' identity verification looks like. There are explicit call-outs around making sure that products and services are inclusive and accessible, and organisations are required to complete an annual exclusion report to transparently explain if certain users are excluded and why.

Extracts from the UK Trust Framework[39]

Make Sure Your Products and Services Are Inclusive

Making your products and services inclusive means everyone can use them no matter who they are or where they're from. One of the aims of the trust framework is to make it as easy as possible for users to create and use digital identities (either online or in person).

All identity service providers must follow the Equality Act 2010 by considering how to make sure no one is excluded from doing this because of

---

[37] https://id4d.worldbank.org/guide/creating-good-id-system-presents-risks-and-challenges-there-are-common-success-factors.

[38] https://www.gov.uk/government/publications/the-uk-digital-identity-and-attributes-trust-framework.

[39] https://www.gov.uk/government/publications/the-uk-digital-identity-and-attributes-trust-framework/the-uk-digital-identity-and-attributes-trust-framework.

their 'protected characteristics'. There are notable exceptions to this, such as it being fair to restrict service access on account of someone's age, e.g., you cannot buy certain products until you are 18.

There are many reasons why a user may be excluded from using a product or service. One common reason is because users are asked to provide specific evidence as proof of their identity.

> Example
>
> A service that only accepts a UK passport as proof of someone's identity will exclude users who do not have, cannot find or cannot afford a passport.

You can prevent this happening by accepting a wide variety of evidence as proof of users' identities and eligibility. You can also choose to accept a declaration from someone that knows the user (known as a 'vouch') as evidence.

Requiring information to be checked against certain authoritative sources can also exclude some users from creating a digital identity.

> Example
>
> A service that only checks users' information against a credit reference agency database will stop users who do not have much of a credit history from creating a digital identity. This could exclude users because of their age or income.

You can prevent this from happening by checking information about users against a wider range of sources.

Another reason why you might exclude users is if a product or service uses any third party software that's only been tested with a specific user group.

> Example
>
> A service might check users' identities using an existing facial recognition system that was tested with a small sample of users. As most of these users

> were white men, the system was not taught how to recognise users of other genders or ethnicities.
>
> By choosing this system, the service will exclude some users from proving their identity because of the way they look.

You can prevent this from happening by choosing software that you know has been tested with a variety of users from different demographics.

The first step to building an inclusive product or service is to find out as much as you can about the types of people who will use it. If you do not know who they are or what they need, you cannot be sure you have built the right product or service.

You must make sure that making your product or service more inclusive will not expose it or your users to any additional risks.

Submit an Annual Exclusion Report

All identity service providers must submit an exclusion report to the governing body every year. The governing body will tell you exactly what information should go in the report. It will at a minimum need to say which demographics have been, or are likely to be, excluded from using your product or service. You must explain why this has happened or could happen.

Sometimes users will be excluded for a good reason. For example, users under 18 should not be able to create a digital identity to access a gambling website so it would be right to stop them from doing this. You must explain if this has happened in the report.

You must write the report based on evidence, for example findings from user research or data and analytics for your product or service. You do not need to collect any additional personal information from your users.

You must also explain what you'll do to improve the inclusion of your product or service in the report.

Make Sure Your Products and Services Are Accessible

You must follow the accessibility regulations if you're a public sector organisation that's developing apps or websites. This includes any products or services that help users create digital identities or manage their attributes.

If you're a public sector organisation that develops products or services for users in Wales, you must also follow the Welsh Language Act 1993. This means your product or service must be available in Welsh.

You should also aim to develop products and services that everyone can use if you're not a public sector organisation. To help do this, we suggest you follow the:

- *Web Content Accessibility Guidelines (WCAG)*
- *new European Telecommunication Standards Institute (ETSI) standard on accessibility requirements suitable for public procurement of ICT products and services in Europe*

You should always make sure users have more than one way to use your product or service. For example, a user should have another way to create a digital identity if they're unable to use the online service.

It is also worth noting that the Information Commissioner in the UK (responsible for upholding information rights in the public interest) has responded in support of the UK Trust Framework, but raises cautions if digital identity and attribute systems (or service providers consuming digital identity and attributes) rely on automated processing, due to use of algorithms or artificial intelligence within the systems. Automated decision making may have discriminatory effects due to bias present in system design, algorithms or datasets used in the creation and build of the product or service.[40]

The Pan-Canadian Trust Framework lists inclusivity as one of its guiding principles, stipulating that digital identity services and tools must be affordable, standardised and create value for users in the interest of broad adoption and benefit to all Canadians.[41]

The World Bank released the second edition of their principles on identification for sustainable development in 2021 to reflect the quickly evolving nature of the identity sector as part of the Identity for Development (ID4D) initiative. The principles are based around three key pillars, the first of which is inclusion. Within this pillar, two key points are called out; (i) *Ensure universal access for individuals, free from discrimination and* (ii) *Remove barriers to access and use*.[42]

At Women in Identity we are currently carrying out a piece of research that seeks to understand the societal and economic impact exclusion in the context of digital identity within the financial services sector.[43] This research

---

[40] https://ico.org.uk/media/about-the-ico/documents/2619686/ico-digital-identity-position-paper-20210422.pdf.
[41] https://diacc.ca/trust-framework/.
[42] https://id4d.worldbank.org/principles.
[43] https://womeninidentity.org/2021/07/13/code-of-conduct-launch/.

will inform the creation of a code of conduct, designed to help solution providers identify and mitigate potential areas of bias and exclusion in digital identity product design, to ensure that the industry is building products that work for everyone, not just the select few.

To conclude, we believe that in order to achieve the full potential of digital identity systems, inclusion requirements must be specifically mandated within any regulation or legislation and measured on an on-going basis. I've mentioned a number of examples of how this is being done elsewhere, and I strongly believe there is benefit in sharing best-practices and lessons learned with other industry bodies and consumer advocacy groups to ensure that we can deliver systems that enable all citizens equally.

Thank you.

Testimony before the U.S. House of Representatives Committee on Financial Services, Task Force on Artificial Intelligence, Hearing on "I Am Who I Say I Am: Verifying Identity while Preserving Privacy in the Digital Age," July 16, 2021, Elizabeth M. Renieris, Professor of the Practice & Founding Director, Notre Dame-IBM Technology Ethics Lab, University of Notre Dame

Introduction

Thank you to Chair Foster, Ranking Member Gonzalez, and members of this Task Force, for the opportunity to testify before you. My name is Elizabeth Renieris. I am a Professor of the Practice and the Founding Director of the Notre Dame-IBM Technology Ethics Lab at the University of Notre Dame, where I help to develop and oversee projects to promote human values in technology. I am also a Technology and Human Rights Fellow at the Carr Center for Human Rights Policy at the Harvard Kennedy School and a Practitioner Fellow at Stanford's Digital Civil Society Lab, where my research is focused on cross-border data governance frameworks, as well as the ethical challenges and human rights implications of digital identity systems, artificial intelligence (AI), and blockchain and distributed ledger technologies (DLT).

My written and oral testimonies reflect my own personal views and do not necessarily reflect those of any organizations with which I am affiliated.

The subject of digital identity is of critical importance to me both personally and professionally. I began my legal career as an attorney working on cybersecurity policy at the Department of Homeland Security and would later learn that my personal information was compromised, alongside the information of more than 22 million other Americans, in the now infamous "OPM hack." More than a decade later, I continue to receive regular alerts from my government-appointed identity monitoring service, notifying me that my social security number, email address, or other information may have been used by an unauthorized party or service.

I went on to practice law on three continents, focused on the data protection and privacy challenges raised by new and advanced technologies, with an emphasis on financial technologies (fintech). As the Founder and CEO of the law and policy consultancy HACKYLAWYER, I have had the opportunity to advise the World Bank, the U.K. Parliament, the European Commission, industry bodies, startups, and a variety of international organizations and NGOs alike, on the intersection of data protection, blockchain, AI, and digital identity. I am also working on a forthcoming book that touches on many of these issues, including the future of digital identity.[44]

I am grateful for the opportunity to participate in a hearing on this important topic and delighted to be joined by esteemed colleagues from organizations which I have actively participated in, including the Better Identity Coalition and Women in Identity.

Digital Identity Is Becoming Critical Infrastructure

Digital identity is often defined as "a collection of electronically captured and stored identity attributes that uniquely describe a [real] person within a given context and are used for electronic transactions."[45] In reality, it is a much more complicated concept with social, technical, political, and economic dimensions.[46] As remote and in-person interactions and transactions

---

[44] Elizabeth M. Renieris, *A Future Beyond Data: A Human Approach to Digital Governance* (MIT Press, 2023).

[45] *See* "Mobile Identity: Enabling the Digital World 2020," *GSMA* (First Ed. January 2020), available at https://www.gsma.com/identity/resources/report-mobile-identity-enabling-the-digital-world (hereinafter "GSMA Report").

[46] Digital identity is a sociotechnical concept with political and economic dimensions. *See* José van Dijck and Bart Jacobs, "Electronic identity services as sociotechnical and political-economic constructs," *New Media and Society*, Vol. 22(5), 896-914 (2020), https://journals-

increasingly have a digital component, such as the use of a smartphone or other device, digital identity is becoming both more ubiquitous and more complex across all dimensions.

As laid bare by the Covid-19 pandemic, we are increasingly reliant on digital tools and services to interact and transact, whether for purposes of work, school, access to healthcare, banking, or government services, and in nearly all aspects of our lives. Unlike when we interact or transact in person, we have limited visibility into who or what is on the other end of a digital interaction or transaction.

Critical infrastructure describes "the physical and cyber systems and assets that are so vital to the United States that their incapacity or destruction would have a debilitating impact on our physical or economic security or public health or safety."[47] Information and communications technology (ICT), energy grids, transportation networks, and financial services are all critical infrastructure. As these sectors are digitized, automated, and algorithmically and computationally manipulated, they increasingly depend on secure digital identity.

Even before the pandemic, vulnerabilities in digital identity systems contributed to everything from election interference[48] to high-profile ransomware attacks, cryptocurrency theft,[49] and network outages, all by exploiting identity-related vulnerabilities. For example, the Colonial Pipeline attackers were able to use a single compromised password to infiltrate a legacy virtual private network (VPN) without multi-factor authentication (MFA) in place.[50]

As we evolve into a world with the "internet in everything" with ever-more internet-of-things (IoT) devices, sensors, networked technologies, and

---

sagepub-com.ezp-prod1.hul.harvard.edu/doi/pdf/10.1177/146144481 9872537.

[47] "Critical Infrastructure Sectors," *Cybersecurity and Infrastructure Security Agency*, https://www.cisa.gov/critical-infrastructure-sectors.

[48] *See* Ellen Nakashima and Shane Harris, "How the Russians hacked the DNC and passed its emails to WikiLeaks," *The Washington Post*, July 13, 2018, https://www.washingtonpost.com/world/national-security/how-the-russians-hacked-the-dnc-and-passed-its-emails-to-wikileaks/2018/07/13/af19a828-86c3-11e8-8553-a3ce89036c78_story.html.

[49] *See, e.g.,* Ellen Nakashima, "U.S. accuses three North Koreans of conspiring to steal more than $1.3 billion in cash and cryptocurrency," *The Washington Post*, February 17, 2021, https://www.washingtonpost.com/national-security/north-korea-hackers-banks-theft/2021/02/17/3dccf0dc-7129-11eb-93be-c10813e358a2_story.html.

[50] *See* Stephanie Kelly & Jessica Resnick-ault, "One password allowed hackers to disrupt Colonial Pipeline, CEO tells senators," *The Verge*, June 8, 2021, https://www.reuters.com/business/colonial-pipeline-ceo-tells-senate-cyber-defenses-were-compromised-ahead-hack-2021-06-08/.

other connected systems, and as the digital becomes the built environment, these vulnerabilities will exponentially increase.[51] Without secure, reliable, and trustworthy digital identities for people, entities, and things, this new cyber-physical reality will subject people and society to attacks, threatening individual safety and national security alike.[52] In this way, *secure digital identity is becoming critical infrastructure.*

At the same time, as dominant technology companies like Google, Apple, Facebook, Amazon, and Microsoft pursue new revenue streams in healthcare, education, financial services, transportation, and more—sectors that include critical infrastructure—the reach of their digital identity infrastructure also expands correspondingly.[53] These companies also exert direct control over the systems and tools needed for digital identity services more generally. For example, with more than 99% of the global market share for smartphone and mobile operating systems combined, Apple and Google's recent introduction of mobile digital identity wallets makes them dominant players in the digital identity space.

Privately owned and operated digital identity systems feature profit-maximizing business models and are driven by commercial incentives that may threaten the privacy, security, and other fundamental rights of individuals and communities.[54] They also tend to incorporate new and advanced technologies, such as AI, machine learning (ML), and blockchain, that are not well understood and often not subject to sufficiently clear legal or governance frameworks. In order to engender trust, safety, and security in the digital ecosystem, we need trustworthy, safe, and secure digital identity. And in order to engender trust, safety, and security in our society, we need to deploy it ethically and responsibly.

---

[51] *See* Laura DeNardis, *The Internet in Everything: Freedom and Security in a World with No Off Switch* (New Haven: Yale University Press, 2020).

[52] *See, e.g.*, Eileen Donahoe, "The Need for a Paradigm Shift on Digital Security," *Centre for International Governance Innovation*, https://www.jstor.org/stable/pdf/resrep05241.10.pdf.

[53] *See, e.g.*, Mike Orcutt, "The radical idea hiding inside Facebook's digital currency proposal," *MIT Technology Review*, June 25, 2019, https://www.technologyreview.com/2019/06/25/800/how-facebooks-new-blockchain-might-revolutionize-our-digital-identities/; Emil Protalinski, "Google is bringing Electronic IDs to Android," *Venture Beat*, May 9, 2019, https://venturebeat.com/2019/05/09/google-is-bringing-electronic-ids-to-android/; Bobby Allyn, "Apple iPhones Can Soon Hold Your ID. Privacy Experts Are On Edge," *NPR*, June 12, 2021, https://www.npr.org/2021/06/12/1005624457/apple-iphones-can-soon-hold-your-id-privacy-experts-are-on-edge.

[54] *See* "Identity Crisis: What Digital Driver's Licenses Could Mean for Privacy, Equity, and Freedom," *ACLU* (May 2021), https://www.aclu.org/news/privacy-technology/digital-ids-might-sound-like-a-good-idea-but-they-could-be-a-privacy-nightmare/.

The Federal Government Must Lead on Standards for Digital Id

Recognizing the growing importance of digital identity as critical infrastructure and seeking to reign in the power of large corporations over it, governments in other countries and jurisdictions, including the European Union, United Kingdom, Canada, Australia, New Zealand, and elsewhere are prioritizing efforts to design and build the infrastructure needed to support robust digital identity.[55]

Not to be confused with mandatory national identity schemes linked to civil registration and vital statistics (CRVS), these are instead digital-first identity solutions that provide a public infrastructure to access digital products and services in the public and/or private sectors. For example, the European Commission has stated, "A universally accepted public electronic identity (eID) is necessary for consumers to have access to their data and securely use the products and services they want without having to use unrelated platforms to do so and unnecessarily sharing personal data with them," acknowledging the importance of providing an alternative to privacy-invasive options like "login with Facebook/Google."[56]

Even as we have hundreds of frameworks for ethical AI principles,[57] we lack any for digital identity systems in particular. In order to remain competitive globally, avoid enclosure of the public sphere through privately owned and operated digital identity infrastructure, and protect the civil and human rights of Americans, the federal government must take the lead in shaping technical, commercial, legal, and ethical standards for the design, development, and deployment of digital identity systems as critical

---

[55] *See* Rob Laurence and Ewan Willars, "A Blueprint for National and International Oversight of the Digital Identity Market," *Open Identity Exchange* (March 2020), https://canada-ca.github.io/PCTF-CCP/docs/RelatedPolicies/Blueprint-for-National-International-Oversight-of-the-Digital-Identity-Market-March-2020.pdf.

[56] *See* "Shaping Europe's Digital Future," *Communication from the Commission to The European Parliament, The Council, The European Economic and Social Committee and The Committee of the Regions*, COM (2020) 67 Final (February 19, 2020), https://ec.europa.eu/info/sites/default/files/communication-shaping-europes-digital-future-feb2020_en_3.pdf.

[57] *See* Jessica Fjeld and Adam Nagy, "Principled Artificial Intelligence: Mapping Consensus in Ethical and Rights-Based Approaches to Principles for AI," *Berkman Klein Center for Internet & Society*, January 15, 2020, https://cyber.harvard.edu/publication/2020/principled-ai.

infrastructure. The *Improving Digital Identity Act* is a good first step in that direction.[58]

Such standards must not only include best practices with respect to the privacy and security of data, but also measures for fairness, transparency, and accountability on the part of entities and organizations designing and deploying the technology, strong enforcement and oversight mechanisms, and adequate remedies and redress for the people impacted. They must also address power asymmetries, the risks of exclusion and discrimination, and specifically address the use of AI, blockchain, and other emerging technologies, by bringing a wide array of voices to the drafting table.

Digital ID Standards Must Address Emerging Technologies

AI/ML in Digital Identity

Emerging technologies such as AI and blockchain are increasingly used in the context of digital identity and access management (IAM), including for identity verification (IDV) and authentication. Verification (or proofing) is typically a one-time process used to onboard a customer or create an account for an individual by linking a unique individual to an identity document or identity information. Authentication is typically a recurring process by which to determine that a previously verified individual is who they say they are on the basis of one or more factors of authentication.

Low assurance environments, like logging into a social media account, may require simple login credentials, such as a username and password. Where more assurance is required, such as accessing a benefits portal, two or more factors may be required, such as login credentials and a code sent to a verified phone number associated with the account. Even higher assurance environments, such as financial services, may require biometrics such as a fingerprint, face, or voice, or (increasingly) behavioral biometrics,[59] many of which are known to exhibit both racial and gender bias.[60]

---

[58] *Improving Digital Identity Act of 2021*, H.R. [ ], 116ᵗʰ Congress (2021), https://foster.house.gov/sites/foster.house.gov/files/Digital%20Identity%20Act%20of%2020 20%20%28FOSTER_065_xml%29.pdf.

[59] *See* GSMA Report, *supra* note 2.

[60] *See* Joan Palmiter Bajorek, "Voice Recognition Still Has Significant Gender Biases," *Harvard Business Review*, May 10, 2019, https://hbr.org/2019/05/voice-recognition-still-has-significant-race-and-gender-biases.

AI and ML systems are frequently used to process biometrics for IAM. For example, remote, AI-powered IDV through the use of biometric facial verification allows individuals to prove their identity by providing an image of their identity documents (e.g., a driver's license or passport) and a live picture or video of their face. Machine learning models are then used to determine the likelihood that those documents are authentic by extracting data from the document and attempting to detect any digital or other manipulations of the photo, such as changes to the name or date of birth. Once the identity document is determined to be authentic, the model is then used to perform a biometric-based facial similarity check to determine whether the facial image on the document matches the face in the selfie or live video of the individual presenting it. If the document is genuine and the faces match, the person passes the IDV check. Machine learning is meant to take these inputs and produce an output at a level that is as good as or better than a human check.[61]

In order to be reliable and accurate, AI-powered digital identity solutions require a lot of data— typically sensitive, personal data such as facial images and other biometrics. A training set of millions of images of faces is required for facial similarity models, which are only as good as the training data and require continuous monitoring and correction.[62] Mistakes in AI used for IDV can lead to significant consequences, such as the denial of access to services, especially when there is no analog or physical alternative, which is increasingly the case. This challenges core data protection and privacy principles such as data minimization, purpose and use limitations, storage limitations, and data integrity and quality principles, among others, while introducing new risks of bias, discrimination, and exclusion.[63]

While we tend to focus on the data privacy and security features of a specific AI-powered ID tool, we often ignore the privacy and security implications for people whose personal data and faces were used to build and train those tools and models in the first place. This creates an asymmetry between the privacy of individuals used as inputs for the AI and the beneficiaries of any tools that incorporate it. Moreover, as a result of complex

---

[61] *See* Neal Cohen, "The Ethical Use of Personal Data to Build AI Technologies: A Case Study on Remote Biometric Identity Verification," *Carr Center Discussion Paper* (April 2020), https://carrcenter.hks.harvard.edu/files/cchr/files/200228_ccdp_neal_cohen.pdf.

[62] *See, e.g.*, Omkar M. Parkhi, Andrea Vedaldi, and Andrew Zisserman, *Deep Face Recognition*, University of Oxford (2015), https://www.robots.ox.ac.uk/~vgg/publications/2015/Parkhi15/parkhi15.pdf.

[63] *See, e.g.*, "Big Data: A Tool for Inclusion or Exclusion: Understanding the Issues," *Federal Trade Commission* (January 2016), https://www.ftc.gov/system/files/documents/reports/big-data-tool-inclusion-or-exclusion-understanding-issues/160106big-data-rpt.pdf.

supply chains of personal data use, the entities designing and building AI-based identity solutions are often not the ones using or deploying them.

Without a direct relationship to the companies designing and building these tools, the chain of responsibility and accountability for privacy and security often breaks down, leaving individuals with limited visibility, control, or recourse over how their information is used.[64] This challenges core data protection and privacy principles, including fairness, transparency, and accountability, among others.

Blockchain/DLT in Digital Identity

Blockchain or DLT is also increasingly being used for IAM activities, including remote IDV and authentication. DLT is a record of transactions that exists and is simultaneously updated on every computer in a network. A blockchain is a subset of DLT in which "blocks" of transactions are cryptographically linked together in a tamper-proof, immutable, append-only record. Communities within standards organizations, such as the World Wide Web Consortium (W3C)[65] and Decentralized Identify Foundation (DIF),[66] and other standards-adjacent groups are working on developing technical standards for blockchain-enabled decentralized identity, sometimes also referred to as self-sovereign identity (SSI).

While the technical specifications are complex and constantly evolving, the basic idea is to use a blockchain or distributed ledger as an authoritative record by which to track and prove ownership over one or more decentralized identifiers (DIDs) through the use of decentralized public key infrastructure (DPKI). These DIDs are then used to manage the exchange of cryptographically verifiable digital credentials consisting of one or more claims about an individual, known as verifiable credentials (VCs).[67] An entity known as an issuer can create or "issue" a VC about an individual (who is the subject of that VC) to a holder, who will "hold" or store the VC in a mobile or

---

[64] This complexity is often compounded by the practice of "white-labeling" or making a technology appear as though it was built and operated by the company making the service available.

[65] W3C DID Working Group, https://www.w3.org/2019/did-wg/.

[66] Decentralized Identity Foundation, https://identity.foundation.

[67] *See* "Verifiable Credentials Data Model 1.0: Expressing verifiable information on the Web," *W3C Recommendation* (November 19, 2019), https://www.w3.org/TR/vc-data-model/#dfn-verifiable-credentials.

web-based digital wallet.[68] Through these wallets (and corresponding wallet software), individuals can use DIDs to establish and manage connections to other individuals and entities, and present VCs to entities who rely on them, known as verifiers.

At its core, blockchain is an accounting technology. It is a transparent, auditable, traceable, and permanent record of transactions, which makes it a popular technology for cryptocurrency and supply chain management.[69] But these same properties make it a high-risk technology to use in connection with personal identity management—*blockchain is anything but private by design*. Conceptually, blockchain remains difficult (if not impossible) to reconcile with core data protection principles such as data minimization (by automatically replicating data across all nodes in a network), storage limitation (by indefinitely storing data), and certain rights related to erasure or the restriction of processing (due to its immutable nature), among others.[70]

To resolve these tensions, blockchain-based identity management relies heavily on various methods of pseudonymization, anonymization, and encryption, particularly for transactional metadata stored on the ledger. Even as new and innovative technical solutions are employed to pseudonymize or anonymize transactional data stored on a distributed ledger, we have countless examples of how inadequate pseudonymization and anonymization techniques can be and how even aggregated, anonymous data can put people and national interests at risk.[71] And even before quantum computing breaks modern

---

[68] The subject and holder may or may not be the same individual. In fact, proving that the holder of a credential is that subject of that credential is one of the biggest unsolved challenges of the decentralized or self-sovereign approach to digital identity.

[69] It is also the backbone of China's central bank digital currency (CBDC), which is legitimately raising concerns about privacy and surveillance. *See, e.g.*, Akram Keram, "China wants to take the entire country cashless—and surveil its citizens even more closely," *The Washington Post*, March 2, 2021, https://www.washingtonpost.com/opinions/2021/03/02/china-digital-yuan-currency-surveillance-privacy/.

[70] *See* Elizabeth M. Renieris, "Forget erasure: why blockchain is really incompatible with the GDPR," *Berkman Klein Center for Internet & Society*, September 23, 2019, https://medium.com/berkman-klein-center/forget-erasure-why-blockchain-is-really-incompatible-with-the-gdpr-9f60374e90f3.

[71] For example, the fitness tracking app Strava made headlines for revealing the location and activities of U.S. military personnel around clandestine bases in Syria when it published anonymized heatmaps of popular running routes. *See* Zack Whittaker, "How Strava's 'anonymized' fitness tracking data spilled government secrets," *ZDNet*, January 29, 2018, https://www.zdnet.com/article/strava-anonymized-fitness-tracking-data-government-opsec/.

encryption,[72] metadata is also increasingly capable of identifying individuals as it gets combined and cross-referenced with other data.

Finally, most blockchain networks still struggle with speed, reliability, and availability.[73] In fact, rather than eliminating single points of failure (as is typically alleged by technology promoters), the blockchain or ledger itself can become an even more pronounced single point of failure in a digital ID system (e.g., if the network is down or transactions cannot be processed, the entire system could malfunction or fail). This is highly problematic from the perspective of digital identity as critical infrastructure.

We Need Guardrails for the Use of Digital Id Systems

Despite the growing ubiquity and importance of digital identity in all facets of life, IAM continues to be a highly technocratic field. Democratic processes and decision-making about the use of emerging technologies for digital identity are often outsourced to technical standards bodies, the private sector, and industry consortia. I have directly participated in many of these groups and I can assure you that they lack all manner of diversity. They are overwhelmingly white, western, and male, and dominated by a veneration for *technical* proficiency (defined as computer science and engineering skills) over and above all other skills, including law and policy expertise. As a result, it can be difficult for the designers and developers of these technologies to imagine or anticipate the risks to people and communities. For example, there tends to be a vast divide between what technologists mean by *privacy* in this context, as compared to how law and policymakers (or the public) think about it.

Privacy is a powerful concept rooted in constitutional and human rights law that has to do with the inviolability of the individual and preventing unlawful interferences with the individual's private life. It is necessary for the exercise and enjoyment of other fundamental rights, including the freedom of thought and conscience, for individual autonomy, and as protection against disparate treatment and discrimination. Unfortunately, in my experience, the

---

[72] *See* Aleksey K. Fedorov, Evgeniy O. Kiktenko, and Alexander I. Lvovsky, "Quantum computers put blockchain security at risk," *Nature*, November 19, 2018, https://www.nature.com/articles/d41586-018-07449-z.

[73] *See, e.g.,* David Floyd, "When Blockchains Go Down: Why Crypto Outages Are on the Rise," *Coindesk*, September 23, 2018, https://www.coindesk.com/when-blockchains-go-down-why-crypto-outages-are-on-the-rise.

technical communities designing and building digital identity standards and systems use the term *privacy* to refer to a kind of mathematical exercise in secrecy and/or anonymity. *Secrecy* in the sense of withholding certain data points in a given interaction or transaction, e.g., industry frequently gives the example of proving that someone is over 21 without revealing their actual date of birth. And *anonymity* in the sense of the degree to which an individual is identifiable or anonymous in a given digital interaction or transaction.[74]

Moreover, digital identity providers often tout their use of zero knowledge proofs or other privacy-enhancing technologies (PETs) in designing and building digital identity solutions. While PETs can be helpful for achieving legal compliance as part of *privacy by design* efforts, many of these technologies and methods remain untested and unproven at scale, while introducing levels of complexity that can actually compromise their stated objectives.[75] As digital identity becomes critical infrastructure, we cannot view *privacy* through such a narrow, mathematical lens. Instead, we must consider the impact of digital identity technologies as part of *complex sociotechnical systems* with serious consequences for individuals, communities, and society at large[76]—repercussions that far exceed the scope of any narrow technical specifications of a single app, tool, or service.

When viewed as part of socio-technical systems, attribute-based identity schemes such as decentralized identity or SSI raise much broader concerns about equity, inclusion, and discrimination, as well as privacy. For example, the data formats and schema used in these systems can determine whether an attribute such as gender is expressed as a mere binary (i.e., male and female) without alternatives. Moreover, when certain attributes are required or encoded, they run the risk of excluding individuals without those attributes. Perhaps less obviously, the use of PETs and the appearance of privacy-preserving design choices can make these systems appear less intrusive, which could make businesses, governments, and other entities feel less restricted to

---

[74] There are also many reasons why an individual might want to share their data, reveal their identity, or otherwise be known in the context of a commercial or non-commercial relationship. Additionally, hiding might be a privilege that is unavailable to those whose access to services is conditioned on sharing personal information or identity information. This is another reason why who is at the table building and shaping these tools and standards matters.

[75] While they can be helpful for achieving legal compliance, privacy-enhancing technologies (PETs) are no panacea and not without significant risks. *See, e.g.*, Elizabeth Renieris, "Why PETs (privacy-enhancing technologies) may not always be our friends," *Ada Lovelace Institute*, April 29, 2021, https://www.adalovelaceinstitute.org/blog/privacy-enhancing-technologies-not-always-our-friends/.

[76] *See* van Dijck and Jacobs, *supra* note 3.

request identity information in contexts where it was previously unacceptable or unnecessary.[77]

When we move through the physical world, we are rarely asked to identify ourselves. Presenting a government-issued ID is the exception, reserved for high-risk situations like boarding an international flight. But as the market for digital ID systems and solutions grows, and as everything from online to in-person services increasingly has a digital component, we are at risk of flipping that paradigm and of requiring people to identify themselves in all manner of settings and situations. Increasingly cheap, efficient, and "seamless" forms of digital identity, such as contactless payments and palm scanning technologies, could also create a fictious need for individuals to identify themselves in contexts where such a need did not previously exist.[78] If we are not careful and deliberate about it, we might go from a situation in which identity is the *exception* to one in which identity becomes the *rule*.

As I argue in a forthcoming book for MIT Press, just because the *data* in a system is private and secure, does not mean that the *people* implicated by the system are protected. For example, just because the data doesn't leave your phone, does not mean you cannot be controlled or manipulated through the use of on-device machine learning algorithms and other computational processes.[79] Reducing the risks of ID systems to questions of mere *data* security and privacy does little to protect the rights of *people*. In fact, it can create a false sense of safety and security that actually puts people at heightened risk. Existing legal frameworks are ill-equipped to address these challenges. To avoid the erosion of privacy through persistent and ubiquitous identification,[80] we will also need to articulate and implement *clear guardrails*

---

[77] *See* Merel Koning, et al, "The ABC of ABC: An Analysis of Attribute-Based Credentials in the Light of Data Protection, Privacy and Identity," *Internet, Law & Politics: A Decade of Transformation* (July 2014), 357-374, http://www.cs.ru.nl/~jhh/publications/abc-of-abcs.pdf.

[78] *See, e.g.*, James Vincent, "Amazon's palm reading starts at the grocery store, but it could be so much bigger," *The Verge*, October 1, 2020, https://www.theverge.com/2020/10/1/21496673/amazon-one-palm-reading-vein-recognition-payments-identity-verification.

[79] *See, e.g.*, Michael Veale, "Privacy is not the problem with the Apple-Google contact-tracing toolkit," *The Guardian*, July 1, 2020, https://www.theguardian.com/commentisfree/2020/jul/01/apple-google-contact-tracing-app-tech-giant-digital-rights.

[80] *See* "Annual Digital Lecture 2020: The death of anonymity in the age of identity," *The National Archives* (February 2, 2021), https://media.nationalarchives.gov.uk/index.php/annual-digital-lecture-2020-the-death-of-anonymity-in-the-age-of-identity/.

around the use of these systems, including when and why identity can be required.[81]

We Need a Public Option That Is Not Driven by Profit Maximization

Right now, there are few commercial incentives around the use of your physical, government-issued identity documents. In general, no one knows when you use them or gets paid when you do (e.g., the DMV isn't typically notified or paid when you use your license to purchase alcohol). In contrast, digital identity schemes typically have commercial and technical incentives that are very different from in-person, manual processes. The use of emerging technologies for digital identity management risks transforming identity from something *relational* (established in the context of government to citizen, or business to customer) into something *transactional*—turning identity into a commodity.

In fact, digital identity is big business and growing bigger every day. The global market for IAM is expected to reach $29.79 billion by 2027,[82] while the global IDV market is expected to reach $17.8 billion by 2026.[83] Cloud-based authentication or identity as a service (IDaaS) offerings based on AI/ML is one of the fastest growing segments of the market.[84] But just as we are learning the high price to society of the targeted behavioral advertising-based business models that fuel social media and the surveillance economy, we must examine the commercial incentives and revenue models behind digital ID schemes.

---

[81] Akin to laws that limit the swiping or scanning of physical drivers licenses by retailers for specified purposes. See, e.g., John T. Cross, "Age Verification in the 21st Century: Swiping Away Your Privacy," 23 J. Marshall J. Computer & Info. L. 363 (2005).

[82] See "Identity and Access Management Market by Component, by Deployment Model, by Application, Competitive Landscape, by Geography and Forecast," *Verified Market Research* (November 2020), available at https://www.verifiedmarketresearch.com/product/global-identity-access-management-market-size-and-forecast-to-2025/.

[83] See "Global Identity Verification Market By Component, By Type, By Enterprise Size, By Deployment Type, By End User, By Region, Industry Analysis and Forecast, 2020 – 2026," *KBV Research* (December 2020).

[84] See "$6.5 Bn Identity as a Service Market – Global Forecast to 2024," *PR Newswire*, September 23, 2019, https://www.prnewswire.com/news-releases/6-5-bn-identity-as-a-service-market---global-forecast-to-2024--300923095.html.

While business models vary, digital identity products and services are typically either enterprise grade (B2B) or consumer grade (B2C). For example, the entity building a remote, AI-based IDV tool is typically a vendor to another company providing a product or service to end users. A common business model in this B2B arrangement is a pay-per-verification scheme, whereby the AI vendor is compensated per verification check (or per query or API call), or per user in a given time frame (e.g., one month) in the case of IDaaS arrangements.[85] Alternative subscriptions and volume-based pricing models, as well as hybrid arrangements are also possible. Certain commercial arrangements, such as pay-per-verification schemes, could incentivize the overuse of identity systems and even undermine the technical features designed to promote privacy.[86]

Coming up with effective business models and commercial incentives for decentralized identity has been one of the core hurdles to adoption of blockchain-based IAM.[87] For example, incentivizing entities to undertake the investment to be able to issue digital credentials may require certain assurances of recouping those costs and extracting value from those credentials. One common solution proposed for this in the SSI context is to have the verifier pay the issuer of a credential for each verification. As with AI-powered IDV, the verifier pay issuer scheme might incentivize overuse and compromise some of the technical measures taken to protect privacy. Moreover, the digital wallet and other software components that intermediate the use of credentials can make it challenging to compensate parties, while ensuring they are blind to what an individual does with those credentials.

---

[85] *See, e.g.*, "Pricing," iDenfy, https://www.idenfy.com/identity-verification-price/.

[86] For example, where a company pays an IDV provider on a pay-per-verification basis and fails to keep personal data separate from billing-related data, this could compromise the privacy and security of data subjects. This is also true with respect to certain decentralized identity solutions and wallet providers that purport to avoid the "phone home" problem at a technical level, while enabling it at a business level.

[87] *See, e.g.*, SSI Ambassador, "The growth factors of self-sovereign identity," *Medium*, April 13, 2020, https://ssi-ambassador.medium.com/the-growth-factors-of-self-sovereign-identity-33aa3cc17ce7.

Finally, leaving access to critical digital identity infrastructure to the private sector risks turning safe, secure, and trustworthy digital identity into a luxury good, as has been the case with privacy.[88] For people without access to or the ability to pay for certain technologies, such as the latest smartphone, the growing ubiquity of digital identity could drive increasing exclusion. And for people with access, it may increase their risk of being surveilled, controlled, and manipulated. To prevent exclusion and avoid predatory inclusion, the government also must ensure the availability of a public option that is shaped by civic and democratic values over and above commercial profit motives.

We Must Prevent Digital Id from Becoming a Tool for Surveillance

Finally, we must avoid building digital identity systems and infrastructure in a way that further expands and entrenches the surveillance state, as do the national identity systems in India or China.[89] Under no circumstances should we think about digital identity as a mandatory, biometric-based national identity scheme, or as an avenue for social credit scoring our citizens. For public schemes, we should avoid the use of a single, centrally-issued, all-purpose, unique identifier for individuals that can be linked across contexts from employment, to education, healthcare, banking, and more.

While we should of course leverage PETs and aim for privacy and data protection by design and default in our digital identity infrastructure, we should not rely on technological solutions alone to address questions of privacy, security, equity, access, and inclusion because identity is inherently sociotechnical. We must also consider the nature of emerging technologies used in digital ID systems, as well as the commercial incentives and impact of business models implicated.

In addition to building consensus around technical, legal, commercial, and ethical standards for digital identity, we also need to articulate and implement concrete guardrails around the use of identity, whether public or private, including when and how ID can be required. Just as privacy is contextual, we must be able to calibrate our use of digital identity infrastructure, depending

---

[88] *See* Adam Clark Estes, "Apple's Newest Luxury Product is Privacy," *Gizmodo*, June 4, 2019, https://gizmodo.com/apples-newest-luxury-product-is-privacy-1835233518.

[89] *See, e.g.*, Nikhil Pahwa, "Thought China was getting all Big Brother? India's not far behind," *Wired*, September 26, 2018, https://www.wired.co.uk/article/india-aadhaar-database-legal-supreme-court.

on the context and circumstances of a given interaction or transaction, as we do in the physical world.

While safe, secure, and trustworthy identity is critical to instill confidence in an increasingly digital world, we must reject the notion that simply using a digital technology or tool should require us to identify ourselves.

Conclusion and Recommendations for Congress

In summary, I would make the following recommendations to Congress when thinking about digital identity policy:

1. We must recognize that digital identity is becoming critical infrastructure, as other countries have acknowledged.
2. While industry is racing ahead, the federal government must lead to create standards for safe, secure, and trustworthy digital identity. The *Improving Digital Identity Act* is a good first step in that direction.
3. Those standards must address specific challenges associated with new and emerging technologies used in these ID systems, such as AI/ML and blockchain/DLT.
4. Regardless of the technologies leveraged, we need guardrails around the use of these ID systems, including when and why ID can be required.
5. We must ensure a public option (akin to the eID in Europe), that is not subject to the same commercial incentives as private digital identity schemes.
6. We must get it right so that digital identity does not become yet another enabler of surveillance and control.

Once again, I appreciate the opportunity to appear before the Task Force and share my perspectives. I look forward to answering any questions you may have.

BLOCKCHAIN ADVOCACY COALITION

Chair Bill Foster and members of the Task Force:

We are writing today on behalf of the Verifiable Credentials Policy Committee of the Blockchain Advocacy Coalition. Similar to other state-level, grassroots organizations, we are a collection of businesses and identity experts who specialize in verifiable credentials and distributed ledger technology. We will limit our comments to **the future of digital identity frameworks, the future of interoperability requirements and standards, and how emerging technologies such as distributed ledger technology could contribute to building a secure and effective digital ID.**

Like several other organizations submitting comments for the record, the Blockchain Advocacy Coalition believes an open standard, called Verifiable Credentials (VCs), as defined by the World Wide Web Consortium (W3C) can serve as the basis of a secure, private and effective digital ID system. This standard was developed by consensus-driven open processes that are publicly observable and subject to public review by any interested party. This standard is at the heart of the discussion and we will center our comments on it but it is worth noting there are many other standards, such as Decentralized Identifiers (DIDs), DID Communications (DIDComm), Linked Data Signature Credentials (JSON-LD), Presentation Exchange, etc. that complement VCs to shape out a complete ecosystem.

Many of these standards were developed with the support of the United States Government and continue to be supported in the Department of Homeland Security (DHS) Science and Technology Directorate Silicon Valley Innovation Program (SVIP)[1], which has been investing in products that use the standards and complete a testing regimen to demonstrate that they are interoperable. In addition, the US Citizenship and Immigration Services (USCIS) is planning on issuing digital Permanent Resident Cards (also known as "green cards") using this technology. The Department of Education is investing in the development of a universal learner wallet that will hold Verifiable Credentials from training and courses from a range of institutions including the military, businesses, colleges, universities, and K-12 schools.

Verifiable Credentials were developed from a digital-first perspective and designed to serve a broad range of use-cases for one entity to assert claims about another. This means it has a very broad expressive capacity and can be adapted by many different business, organizational and government entities.

What is wrong with the earlier digital identity architectures?

You are probably familiar with the legacy architecture as it exists on the internet today via "login-with" features, such as "Login with Google/Facebook/etc". This system is so pervasive on the web that the world's largest technology companies have become the default intermediaries

BLOCKCHAIN ADVOCACY COALITION

for people's digital selves. In practice, this position as identity intermediary grants these companies a broad set of rights to observe and monetize an individual's online activity in ways that could exploit the user. There is mounting evidence that this architecture is disempowering to individual users, and gives those large "identity providers" too much power over people's digital selves. It also creates a vendor lock-in for their services that only exacerbates their potentially monopolistic power.

This legacy pattern is similar to architectures like those proposed by ISO 18013f for mobile drivers licences (mDLs) which is currently being considered by the American Association of Motor Vehicle Administrators (AAMVA). This proposed standard, largely developed with AAMVA participation, creates a centralized, digital intermediary architecture that requires the mDL holder to continuously validate their identity with the mDL identity service provider. This effectively creates a digital trail of "breadcrumbs" where a person who uses their ID potentially exposes every activity to government servers and records. While this approach is familiar to practitioners, and by extension popular, we believe it's adoption would extend the proliferation of an obsolete technical infrastructure requiring unnecessary costs in the future.

These privacy concerns are one of the reasons governments including Canada and its Provinces, the US Government, and members of the European Union (especially Germany and The Netherlands)are active in developing standards, industry consortia, and building products with verifiable credentials technology.

How Verifiable Credential digital identity architecture is different than the legacy

Verifiable Credentials have privacy enhancing capabilities that are in alignment with the legal frameworks and ethical values of these governments because digital identity is considered an inherent right of the citizen, including the rights to consent before sharing their identity and revoke it at their discretion. The EU's recent announcement [2] about a digital wallet initiative has potential political traction, in part because it provides an open standards path away from the market control (via identity control) that is dominated by the proprietary technologies of the major technology companies today.

Verifiable Credentials are an innovation in identity technology that means the identity provider becomes a credential issuer and the verifier, the entity formerly known as the relying party, becomes a credential verifier. **Though verifiable credentials often use blockchain or distributed ledger technology, AT NO POINT is personal information recorded on the blockchain**. The individual holder of the credential is the pivot point of connection and integration - not the state, private company, or other third party service provider. An individual is issued (or self-generates) a verifiable credential that they hold and then share a verifiable presentation with any verifier they choose without surveillance. The verifier checks the cryptographic signatures and ensures validity of the credential and that it came from the issuer.

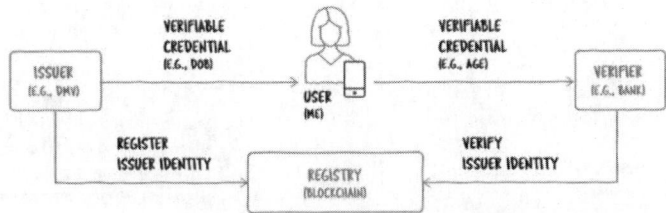

In the two years since the specification was completed, a particular flavor of this standard has emerged [3] that supports a selective disclosure, a privacy enhancing technology that gives individuals the capacity to share a subset of attributes on any credential. For example if a person only needs to share their year of birth instead of all the attributes that were on the credential signed by the issuer they can because each statement is separately signed by the issuer.

California Verifiable Credentials Legislation

California's state government has been exploring verifiable credentials. The independent and industry expert-led Blockchain Working Group, which was established under the Governor's Government Operations Agency recommended several use cases for this technology including: benefits distribution, DMV operations, and securing health records.

The Blockchain Advocacy Coalition sponsored AB 2004 in 2020 which would have confirmed that verified credentials are an acceptable form of test results and created a working group to develop standards for their use.

For COVID-19 test results, verifiable credentials would work quite simply: a California resident could get tested and request that the doctor send them a verifiable credential to confirm their result. The doctor could use a verifiable credential platform to send the result, and the resident would most likely receive it on their smartphone as an electronic barcode, also known as a QR code. They could then use that code to enter a salon, workplace or anywhere they wish to share their test result.

Other Government Uses

Other governments have moved ahead with pilots to prove the promise of these technologies. The UK National Health Service (NHS) has been issuing VCs to help medical professionals prove validity of their licenses at hospitals, using the Sovrin Ledger. The British Columbia Verifiable Organizations Network (VON) has issued registrations, permits and licenses for 10,000's of companies in BC since 2019.

This committee should consider digital identity as a piece of the interoperable world of data and privacy we have today. While pilots and individual use cases are effective for proof of concept, we urge this committee to consider the implementation of a Trust Framework. A trust framework would provide uniform and interoperable standards for the use of this technology across public and private applications. It would avoid monopolies and vendor lock-in, and allow America's ecosystem of innovators to create solutions for tomorrow's identity problems that afford greater privacy to our citizens.

Thank you for your consideration.

Best,

Ally Medina, Director *Blockchain Advocacy Coalition*
Kaliya Young, Chair *Verifiable Credentials Policy Committee*

[1] DHS Science and Technology Directorate Silicon Valley Innovation Program "Interoperability Plugfest #2" VC/DID Multi-Platform/Multi-Vendor Interoperability Showcase/Demo March 18, 2021
https://docs.google.com/presentation/d/1MeeP7vDXb9CpSBfjTybYbo8qJfrrbrXCSJa0DklNe2k/edit#slide=id.p1

[2] Digital Identity for all Europeans by the European Commission
https://ec.europa.eu/info/strategy/priorities-2019-2024/europe-fit-digital-age/european-digital-identity_en

[3] Verifiable Credential Flavors Explained, by Kaliya Young "Identity Woman" published by Linux Foundaiton Public Health
https://www.lfph.io/wp-content/uploads/2021/02/Verifiable-Credentials-Flavors-Explained.pdf

I Am Who I Say I Am

U.S. House Financial Services Committee Task Force on Artificial Intelligence

"I Am Who I Say I Am: Verifying Identity while Preserving Privacy in the Digital Age"
Rev. Ben Roberts, Foundry United Methodist Church
July 16, 2021

Chairman Foster, Ranking Member Gonzalez, and members of the committee,

Thank you for the opportunity to submit a written statement on the topic of identity verification. I write to express the experience and stories of the volunteers and clients of Foundry United Methodist Church's ID Ministry. The ID Ministry is a 20-year-old initiative of Foundry Church that assists unhoused and low-income residents of Washington, D.C. and the immediate metro region navigate and pay for critical documents as they seek to secure their Non-Driver's IDs.

As the Task Force, Financial Services Committee, and tech and financial services community seek to build strong policy and systems, my testimony is meant to service as a reminder **that our systems must remain accessible lest we repeat the mistakes of our current paper credentialling systems.**

Each week, ID Ministry volunteers and clients repeatedly experience barriers and roadblocks in obtaining the vital documents they need to do things like apply for jobs, obtain housing, and register their children for school. As you craft new policies and more secure systems, our hope is that you give attention to the need for multiple routes of attainment, so that individuals — particularly vulnerable ones — aren't inadvertently kept out of the very systems with which many are encouraging them to engage (e.g. banking).

Through ID Ministry, Foundry Church offers assistance to low-income and unhoused persons who need help obtaining their Non-driver's IDs or Birth Certificates. We are assisting approximately 2,000 guests each year with an all-volunteer staff. Since the implementation of the new Real ID standards, the process for obtaining an ID has become increasingly cumbersome and often prohibitive for those who are starting from nothing.

If a person comes to Foundry and has no documentation, often due to it being stolen, lost, or damaged, the process is as follows:

- Come to Foundry to work with our volunteers
- Get a medical record signed by a doctor
- Use that medical record to get a social security card (which is mailed),
- Use those records, with other documents, to get a birth certificate
- Take all of those, plus two proofs of residency and a check from Foundry, to the DMV
- The ID is then mailed, often within two weeks
- This process averages a month or more.

This is the process most people will face if they do not have access to a lawyer or case worker who can fast track the process. Many of the people we see are without support, with no one able or willing to vouch for them. Usually, our guests have been working unsuccessfully for multiple weeks – sometimes months – before finding us.

The cost for the ID and Birth Certificate in DC is $43 total ($23 for the certificate, though it varies by state; $20 for the non-driver's ID). Add that to the cost of transportation (consider a $5 round trip x 5 different stops = $25). This puts the cost to the individual at about $68. Now, add to that the costs incurred by taking time off of work or obtaining child care to attend these appointments.

Pandemic adjustments

For ID Ministry volunteers, the Covid-19 pandemic has meant limited in-person service. We have tried to fill gaps by establishing a process for over-the-phone assistance and coaching. Unfortunately, all guests must have case workers, which means we miss people who aren't able to take that step.

During the pandemic, the process of obtaining these documents became even longer, with more mailings, increased delays, and longer waits for DMV appointments. To make matters worse, there was no in-person service at DC Vital records, which lead to dramatic cost increases (65% per birth certificate in DC). This same lack of in-person service existed at the Social Security Office. **Regardless of pandemic protocols, every delay and return trip for additional documentation means lost wages, lost employment opportunities, lost housing opportunities, and delays for enrolling in education opportunities.**

Here are a few examples of what we see through our work. Names have been changed to protect the identities of ID Ministry clients.

Example Scenario 1: Occurred in 2021

"Jason" is a university student who is experiencing homelessness. He did not know either of his parents growing up, and lived with an extended family member who passed away during his final year of high school. Jason currently has a residence through his university housing, and was able to obtain a verification letter from his school's homeless liaison. The goal of Jason's visit was to get a DC ID so that he could open a bank account.

Currently, Jason cashes his employment checks at a check cashing store. His larger checks, such as his 2020 stimulus check and a refund from his university, had remained uncashed as he was scared to carry that much cash.

Jason came to ID Ministry with two proofs of DC residency: 1. his cell phone bill and 2. a letter from his university proving that he lived on campus. Unfortunately, he was not able to prove his social security number to the current system. Jason's paystub from his employer only lists the last four digits of his social security number. ID Ministry tried to assist him in getting a new social security card, he didn't have the credit history to complete the online prompts.

When we called to inquire about the steps for mailing in an application for a social security card, we were told to send in a birth certificate, a medical record, and the application. Jason actually had his birth certificate — but it contained a typo in his first name. We called the Social Security Office, and confirmed they also have the name "*Jasoa*" on file instead of "Jason," and thus a replacement social security card was not an available route to prove that he had a social security number. We decided to wait until he received his 2020 W-2 from his employer. But when the W-2 arrived, it also didn't have the full social, just the last four digits. Jason called his employer to see if it can be reissued with the full number, was told *no* for "security purposes."

Since he was not converting a license from out of state, but instead getting a new one, there was also a need to present a birth certificate. But the birth record also contained an error. So, even with the documents on hand — proof of residency, letters from social workers, and letters from the university — he still didn't have the combination needed to obtain his documents. And since the birth record contained an error, the documents on hand did not match his birth certificate on record.

We were first contacted by Jason on January 3, 2021. He received his amended birth certificate on June 3, 2021. It took nearly six months just getting him to a place where he could start the process to amend his social security record. All the while, the primary goal of opening a bank account went unfulfilled. Stimulus checks went uncashed until the last minute, and a large percentage ended up with the check cashing store.

Other experiences from our clients:

1. "Mr. Lawrence:" Mr. Lawrence needed the birth certificate to get into sheltered senior housing in DC.[1] His birth certificate was not in the name he used all his life. He in New York City to unwed parents, his mother's name (Miles) was listed as his surname per NYC statute, but he used his father's name from infancy (Lawrence). All his records — school, employment, etc. — were in the name Lawrence, so NYC wouldn't issue his birth certificate in the name Miles. Eventually, he had to go to DC court and have his name legally changed to Lawrence, then NYC issued an amended birth certificate. This ended up being nearly a three-year process.

2. "Mr. Watts:" Mr. Watts needed birth certificate to obtain social services. Born in Georgia in the 1960s, his birth took place at home and he never had a birth certificate as his mother was turned away when she tried to register him. At the time, Georgia county clerks were allowed to decide what births to register (Mr. Watts is Black). We were able to get Army records, VA records, marriage records, genealogy records, and even school records, and eventually got Georgia to issue a delayed birth certificate.

3. A woman has fled domestic violence with her two young children, with nothing but the clothes on their backs. She needed to restore all their documents to get the kids into school, get a job, get housing, and open a bank account.

---

[1] https://www.washingtonpost.com/lifestyle/magazine/what-happens-to-people-who-cant-prove-who-they-are/2017/06/14/fc0aaca2-4215-11e7-adba-394ee67a7582_story.html

These cycles we see tend to rotate around the need to have one document to get another, layered with slow transactional relationships born of crisis. These are not the ideal or average user experience in mind when policies are made, but they're real and prevalent, nonetheless.

You as policy writers and system developers have a massive task before you of trying to secure data and authenticate and verify identities. **My charge to you is to be intentional in your development of these policies and systems, mindful of the harm that can arise by not having reasonable insight into the ways people have to interact with these requirements for identification.**

Reliable digital identity process can likely overcome some challenges faced by our clients. Being able to remotely prove one's identity can eliminate extra trips our clients take, going back and forth to brick-and-mortar agencies, but this benefit can be hampered by online fees. If there's a reliable recovery process, it can assist clients who see their paper documents destroyed by rain, fire, theft, or lost while sleeping on the street or being caught in an eviction process.

The right processes could eliminate the need of clients to approach abusive partners or parents who often restrict access to documents in their procession as a means of control or simply because of the broken relationship. It could assist in the renewal or recovery process by speeding up the timeline and eliminating waiting periods. Acts of investment can tackle some of the cost associated with moving through the identity process. However, none of those things can happen or help unless the policies and systems are built in such a way that people can successfully complete it, even on their worst day.

As you work to craft policy, I remind you that these requirements become real barriers to housing, employment, and education. For those of you also developing systems, remember that the average user experience is just that — average. Those interfacing with systems in crisis situations may not be large compared to our overall population, but they are in critical and often desperate situations. If you fail to make systems that are nimble enough to handle the unexpected or lack avenues of feedback, you will do unintentional harm.

All of you have power and agency to explore the unconsidered and become leaders in the creation of socially conscious and more virtuous products and processes.

I sincerely extend an invitation to any who would like to come to Foundry United Methodist Church to see the work of ID Ministry and better understand the challenges your neighbors are facing as they attempt to navigate the broken system that's been created.

In peace,

Rev. Ben Roberts

Associate Pastor
Director of Social Justice Ministries
Foundry United Methodist Church

1500 16th St. NW
Washington, D.C. 20036
Phone: 202-332-4010
Fax: 202-332-4035

I am Chair of the Board of the Texas Blockchain Council and Chair of the TBC's Digital Identity Committee. I have been notified that you are accepting written testimony for the upcoming virtual hearing, "I Am Who I Say I Am: Verifying Identity while Preserving Privacy in the Digital Age." Below please find my testimony.

What if each individual could be their own database? Let's imagine a world where, instead of giant centralized databases storing millions of data points about millions of people, each individual is a custodian of their own personal data, and they decide who gets access to that data, for how long, and for what purpose. For example, instead of Facebook storing my data, I store my data myself and lend it out to Facebook if I choose. Then, when I want to, I can revoke Facebook's access to that data, and they are technically prevented from using it ever again.

If we can build such a world, then hackers will have a much more challenging assignment: instead of hacking one centralized database that contains millions of people's personally-identifiable information, they would have to hack millions of individual databases, one at a time.

What would make hacking or improper use of personal data even more difficult? If knowing one piece of information about someone couldn't "unlock" any other information about that person--for example, if you know my social security number, that doesn't give you any special access to any other information about me. Instead of using identifying information, I get access to my accounts through cryptographic verification of my own identity.

This world is not imaginary: it is being built right now by communities working on new technical standards for verifiable credentials. These standards are creating a "private identity layer" for the World Wide Web--enabling people to own their data and protect it against unauthorized and malicious use.

These new digital identity standards employ advanced cryptography and blockchain technology to provide the highest level of certainty about identity--enabling me to prove that I really am who I say I am--without divulging anything unnecessary about myself. This technology enables me to prove all kinds of things--like my age, the school I graduated from, my birthdate, my address--without revealing any more data than I absolutely need to, and without correlating that data to any other data about me. Then, once I've proven I am who I say I am, I can revoke access to that identity data.

The Federal Government has a role to play in ensuring that these new data standards be adopted: it can set policy and write regulations that encourage the use of verifiable credentials and adjacent technical standards. It can provide grants and other funding to organizations building these standards. In procurement, it can write RFP requirements and prefer vendors that use these open standards over those who use closed, proprietary identity verification solutions.

I am happy to answer any questions the House Financial Services Committee may have about these new standards and how they will create more security, privacy, and peace of mind for millions of Americans.

All my best,

--
Natalie Smolenski
Head of Business Development
Hyland Credentials
(c) (972) 358-5542

The Honorable Bill Foster
Chairman, Task Force on Artificial Intelligence
House Committee on Financial Services

Dear Congressman Foster,

The Trust over IP (ToIP) Foundation thanks you for the opportunity to provide comments for the record in support of the Task Force hearing, "**Virtual Hearing - I Am Who I Say I Am: Verifying Identity while Preserving Privacy in the Digital Age**"

As you have previously heard in testimony to the Task Force, digital identity has been not only increasingly convenient in today's world, but offers the opportunity to provide tremendous advancements in convenience and accessibility to online services. However, verifying digital identity while preserving privacy has become increasingly challenging, especially with artificial intelligence. To quote the testimony of Ms Valerie Abend of Accenture, a ToIP founding member company, "Simply put, identifying yourself online through passwords, usernames, and security questions is no longer working." These challenges serve as the basis for the global focus on the use of digital identity standards such as verifiable credentials (VCs) and decentralized identifiers (DIDs).

ToIP was launched in May 2020 as an independent project hosted by the Linux Foundation. As such, ToIP itself is a relatively new contributor in the area of VCs, DIDs, and decentralized digital trust infrastructure. Nevertheless, today ToIP members *include over 240 leading companies, organizations and individual contributors* sharing expertise and defining standards and specifications to advance a secure and privacy-preserving trust layer for the digital world. ToIP members bring extensive experience and expertise to the task of defining a complete architecture for Internet-scale digital trust that combines cryptographic trust at the machine layer with human trust at the business, legal, and social layers.

In order to enable trusted transactions and relationships online, digital credentials need to be grounded in governance frameworks that spell out the business, legal, and technical rules under which they operate. This is how ToIP proposes to move beyond the mere technology of digital identity: by integrating governance as a first-class component. We believe that applications that foster digital trust must begin with a clear understanding of their business requirements, then move to regulatory and policy requirements that are transparently communicated in complete governance frameworks. Only at this stage—when the parameters for creating real human trust are fully articulated—can the technology components be selected to implement a successful solution in the market.

ToIP aims to break from the thousands of siloed solutions for digital identity and credential issuance that do not work with each other. This lack of interoperability potentially costs billions of dollars per year in complicated and time-consuming integration and hinders adoption by the very customers they purport to serve. Our goal is to drive adoption of a new model for digital trust that is every bit as interoperable as the physical wallets and paper or plastic credentials that we use every day—to do everything from getting on a plane to entering a hospital to signing a mortgage.

As these new tools emerge, they will become as essential to our digital lives as browsers and email clients have become to the Web today. Interoperable solutions are paramount for a vibrant digital marketplace where consumers are free to choose the vendors and use the digital credentials they prefer. The goal of the ToIP Foundation is to define a complete architecture that will do for interoperable Internet-scale digital trust what the original Internet architecture did for interoperable data exchange.

We believe this architecture—the ToIP stack—can be an extremely useful architectural and governance tool for the work of this Task Force, especially for the preservation of privacy relative to digital identity and digital trust relationships. We are happy to assist the Task Force in further explaining it in any way that will be helpful.

Note that the Foundation's mission is not to develop all of the standards or components included in the ToIP stack. Rather it is to specify how these elements can be combined to fulfill the requirements of all four layers, integrating technology and governance at each layer. The ToIP Foundation works closely with other standards development organizations (SDOs), industry foundations, and consortia to combine their open standards, architectures, and protocols into a complete, consensus-driven and coherent stack for Internet-scale digital trust.

For more complete background on the ToIP Foundation and the ToIP stack, please refer to our founding whitepaper provided with this letter.

Thank you for your consideration,

John Jordan
Executive Director
The Trust over IP Foundation

TESTIMONY OF SHAMSH HADI
CEO OF ZORROSIGN, INC.

BEFORE THE U.S. HOUSE COMMITTEE ON FINANCIAL SERVICES TASK FORCE ON ARTIFICIAL INTELLIGENCE

HEARING ON "I AM WHO I SAY I AM: VERIFYING IDENTITY WHILE PRESERVING PRIVACY IN THE DIGITAL AGE"

JULY 16, 2021

Chair Foster and Ranking Member Gonzalez — thank you for affording me the opportunity to submit testimony to the Task Force on Artificial Intelligence as part of the Task Force's hearing on verifying identity while preserving privacy in the digital age. My name is Shamsh Hadi and I am the CEO of ZorroSign, Inc. - a company based in Phoenix, AZ. ZorroSign is the pioneer of electronic signature technology and the developer of ZorroSign DTM, a unified platform, a complete Electronic Signature and Digital Transaction Management solution. ZorroSign's unique Document 4n6 (forensics) technology offers post-execution fraud detection and verification and authentication of electronic signatures and documents using blockchain tokenization. I am also a founder member of the Association of Data and Cyber Governance (ADCG).

As the CEO of a company that lives and breathes consumer data privacy and security, I am pleased to offer this testimony on how an emerging technology such as blockchain can and should be an essential component to the ongoing efforts to create high quality and privacy-preserving secure digital identity (ID).

According to a paper issued in February of 2019 by the National Institute of Standards and Technology (NIST Annual Manufacturing Series 300-6), *"blockchain is a distributed storage framework that is virtually tamper resistant, has a native synchronization-discrepancy-resistance mechanism and is already highly praised in the financial world."*

In its simplest form, blockchain is a shared fixed ledger for recording transactions. The concept of blockchain can and has been extended to have the highest levels of security and privacy protecting the sensitive information and identities of authorized individuals in a network who have permission to access the content stored in the ledger.

Blockchain is a digital record where all transactions are recorded in the order of occurrence and where the next record is linked and related to the previous record. It is a continuous database of records that can only be added to and never edited or deleted. In layman's terms, blockchain allows government agencies and businesses to secure and validate a digital asset, like a contract, enabling the enforcement of ownership or authenticity.

The noteworthy characteristics of a blockchain are:

- Indelible: The most important and distinctive property of blockchain. Once a transaction is written into a block, it can never be erased or modified by anyone, including the person who wrote the transaction.

- Globally Readable: Anyone who has permission to view the transaction can read what it contains and everyone sees exactly the same content.

- Accept Rules Based Rights: Any chosen party can write into the blockchain if it respects the predetermined rules set out for that transaction.

- Strictly Ordered: There is no ambiguity of the transaction. The audit trail will clearly show which block of data came first and which came second.

In its February 2019 paper, NIST noted that because blockchain *"...is tamper resistant and the blocks are timestamped, a blockchain is a robust solution to prove the existence of a specific asset at a certain time during the product lifecycle"* and *"a safe way to track both the existence and ownership of a digital asset at a certain time."*

In addition to keeping track of and protecting Personally Identifiable Information (PII) or a person's digital identity, there are a plethora of practical applications of blockchain in the real world:

- Banking: Financial transactions from opening an account to money transfers.
- Health care: Medical records and drugs composition.
- Real Estate: Track real estate transactions and tracking maintenance and upgrade of properties.
- Supply Chain Management: Tracking food supply from "farm to dining table."
- Contract management: Chain of Custody, Audit trail, and entitlement tracking.
- Retail: Protect consumers against issues of product authenticity. Using blockchain retail consumer goods can be tracked, eliminating the risk of consumers receiving counterfeit goods.
- Electronic Voting: Voter registration, personal identity, and voting records.
- Diamond Industry: Using immutable tamper proof digital ledger, record: color, carat, certificate number (inscribed by laser on the crown or girdle of the stone), and origin in

order to increase supply chain efficiency and eliminate conflict diamonds from market. Makes it possible to track diamond from origin to consumer.

Please note that blockchain is NOT Bitcoin. Cryptocurrency like Bitcoin uses blockchain, but they are not the same. Blockchain is not cryptocurrency or Bitcoin. Rather, Bitcoin uses blockchain to secure transactions and publicly record them in a distributed ledger.

Blockchain is important because it has unique qualities that set it apart from other transaction database management systems. Specifically, blockchain is being used today in private, permissions-based decentralized systems that are secure, trusted and automated with bank grade security. Ultimately, blockchain technology helps make digital transactions more secure, faster and less expensive.

One of the conclusions of the February 2019 NIST paper was that *"Due to its tampering resistance, blockchain is an ideal candidate to record and secure data exchanges."* As someone who has spent the better part of my career working on and with blockchain, I wholeheartedly agree with NIST's conclusion.

In terms of possible legislative action, the bill that Chair Foster introduced last month, H.R. 4258, the *Improving Digital Identity Act of 2021*, represents an important step in the right direction. Enactment of this bill into law will ensure that the United States remains a world leader when it comes to online privacy and security. Indeed, the future of our economy depends on the U.S. government tackling this issue and doing everything possible to ensure that the United States is on the cutting edge when it comes to digital identity verification services.

The Task Force may also want to consider ensuring that any legislation that sets national standards for consumer user privacy and data security require that any business or government entity that collects a consumer's Personal Identifiable Information (PII) have in place systems, products and services that ensure the privacy and security of that consumer's personal information and their data.

Such systems, products and services should prevent the unauthorized view/review, re-distribution and modification of personal information, and to the greatest degree possible:

1) Utilize Digital Security Certificates that never expire;

2) Employ blockchain tokenization technology to tamper-seal and verify actual users and authenticate documents and data, without the need for third-party authentication;

3) Ensure unbroken chain-of-custody of all consumer personal information and documents;

4) Provide a clear audit trail for every transaction that includes consumer personal information and/or documents;

5) Use a secure method of digital signatures if consumers are required to sign documents.

6) Employ authentication and user identity verification that does not rely on password-based log-in protocols, but instead employs biometrics or hardware tokens.

7) Replace password-based security verification with proof of identity via uniquely identifiable methods such as knowledge-based authentication, one-time password

generator, Trusted device, hardware token, or the user's biometric signature (e.g. fingerprint, face, retina, etc.).

Any federal framework on data privacy that does not include the above requirements and recommendations would fall short of what is needed to fully protect consumer data and ensure the integrity of digital transactions — both in the public and private sectors. The thoughtful and intentional employment of blockchain to safeguard personal data is one way to achieve the dual goal of protecting consumers while at the same time preserving the economic and social benefits of data. In my view, blockchain represents a viable solution for many of the challenges facing both our country and the global community when it comes to digital identity, privacy and combating identity theft. At the very least, blockchain needs to be one of several emerging technologies that can and should be employed to better verify digital identity and preserve privacy.

Thank you for your time and consideration. I would be happy to answer any questions the Task Force members might have, either in person or in writing.

Advancing Convenience & Fuel Retailing | convenience.org

July 15, 2021

The Honorable William Foster
Chairman
Artificial Intelligence Task Force
    Financial Services Committee
U.S. House of Representatives
2129 Rayburn House Office Bldg
Washington, DC 20515

The Honorable Barry Loudermilk
Ranking Member
Artificial Intelligence Task Force
    Financial Services Committee
U.S. House of Representatives
2129 Rayburn House Office Bldg
Washington, DC 20515

Dear Chairman Foster and Ranking Member Loudermilk:

    Thank you for holding a hearing on verifying identity and preserving privacy in the digital age. The National Association of Convenience Stores (NACS) and its members have struggled with these topics for years.

    NACS is an international trade association representing the convenience industry with more than 1,500 retail and another 1,500 supplier companies as members, the majority of whom are based in the United States. The industry employed about 2.34 million workers and generated more than $548.2 billion in total sales in 2020, representing nearly 3 percent of U.S. gross domestic product. The industry processes more than 160 million transactions every single day. That means about half of the U.S. population visits our members on a daily basis. In fact, ninety-three percent of Americans live within 10 minutes of one of our locations. The average time a customer spends in one of our stores is about three and one-half minutes and the industry is focused on ensuring that the customer's needs are met as efficiently as possible – saving them time and money.

NACS has led efforts to restrict youth access to age-restricted products for the past half century:

- 1971: NACS introduced the c-store industry's first age-verification training video
- 1985: NACS kicked off the national launch of "I.D. Please: It's the Law" program to prevent sales of alcohol to minors
- 1990s: NACS was a founding member of the We Card program, providing employee training and educational programs that prevent age-restricted product sales to minors and promote responsible retailing, consistently driving down youth availability in retail. We Card is supporting NACS in its effort to bring TruAge™ to market.
- 2010: NACS supported enactment of the Prevent All Cigarette Trafficking (PACT) Act, which regulates the online sale and delivery of tobacco products and closed loopholes for minors to acquire tobacco products
- 2020: NACS supported enactment of the Preventing Online Sales of E-Cigarettes to Children Act. The law requires online e-cigarettes sellers to ensure delivery carriers verify the age of recipients upon delivery.

The volume of transactions that the convenience store industry quickly processes is impressive; at the same time stores also need to ensure that all sales are conducted legally and responsibly. About 50 percent of all transactions inside convenience stores (which don't include fuel transactions) include an age-restricted product like alcohol, tobacco, lottery tickets, and others. Convenience stores are leaders in age verification: Convenience stores sell around 32 percent of all age-restricted items in the United States. With that in mind, the industry has made it a priority to continually improve its ability to verify the age of purchasers – and to do so while respecting and protecting their privacy.

The latest result of those industry efforts is TruAge™, a groundbreaking digital identification solution that enhances current age-verification systems at retail points of sale and protects user privacy. NACS worked with its standards-setting partner, Conexxus, and Digital Bazaar, a recognized leader in open standard digital identity, to develop TruAge™. The system uses a customer's date of birth and photo to verify identity. When confirming age and identity, one-time-use tokens are placed on the customer's mobile device to confirm legal age to purchase age-restricted products. With payments and commerce going digital, TruAge™ uses the technology to verify the age of purchasers of age-restricted products.

A standard driver's license contains 33 separate lines of information that can be accessed in current age verification practices. Importantly, TruAge™ only shares 4 of them: the user's name, date of birth, photo, and whether the ID is current or expired – none of this information can be used to identify the consumer without access to the appropriate DMV data base. That makes it effective while minimizing privacy and data security risks.

This allows for reliable verification of age while maximizing the protection of privacy and minimizing any risk of data theft – a key societal challenge in the digital future. The system works for all types of purchases from in-person transactions to those conducted on the Internet and via mobile apps.

And, TruAge™ is an open-standard age-verification solution. It is free to retailers, consumers and point-of-sale providers. In our view, widespread consumer and business adoption is important to the value and reliability of this solution. Therefore, all relevant intellectual property will be placed in the public domain in order to remove barriers to adoption.

This is the model of what reliable verification systems that respect privacy can look like. By describing it below, we hope that this provides the Committee with useful background that will help foster public policy supporting this type of solution to everyone's benefit.

How TruAge™ Works

There are a couple of different ways that age can be verified by the TruAge™ system. For example, when a customer is purchasing an age-restricted product(s), the checkout process is similar to the traditional carding approach, but faster, safer, and more reliable. What happens is:

1. After the cashier scans an age-restricted item, the point-of-sale system prompts for verification of age – the system will not let the cashier proceed without a verification.

2. The cashier then scans the barcode on the back of the customer's driver's license and does a visual check to ensure that the person making the purchase matches the ID.

3. Finally, the system confirms that the customer is old enough to make the purchase, sending a randomly generated, single-use token that serves as validation of a verified age. It's also a reference for forensically determining "who" purchased the item. This is a safeguard built into the program in

the rare case that law enforcement needs to determine who made the purchase, and as a deterrent to social sourcing to youth; the biggest contributor to underage use.

Alternatively, a store may have an app that integrates with TruAge™ or the store may use the TruAge™ app. In these cases what happens is:

1. After the cashier scans an age-restricted item, the point-of-sale system prompts for verification.

2. The customer opens the app on their smartphone to unlock a single-use QR code for the cashier to scan.

3. Finally, the system confirms that the customer is old enough to make the purchase, sending a randomly generated, single-use token that serves as validation of a verified age.

4. This feature is also available for the consumer to use online, with TruAge compliant websites; enabling a fast and cost-effective means to verify age for all mobile and online occasions.

TruAge™ incorporates emerging industry standards on identity championed by the World Wide Web Consortium, Department of Homeland Security SVIP program, and other standards-setting bodies to assure privacy while increasing reliability of age verification. Most importantly, it preserves the relationship between the consumer and identity issuer without the risk of a private third party having to be involved, therefore returning identity control to the consumer.

The system uses ID-validation and age-calculation procedures that are not available with a standard ID card. The digital version of TruAge™ provides single-use digital tokens that eliminate all personal information needed to verify age in any transaction—a capability that satisfies emerging privacy regulations and reduces the risk of identity theft.

Protecting Privacy

TruAge™ has been designed with privacy in mind. The only personal information stored in the database is a "token" (a randomly generated code) of a customer's age. Because it is a token, it is useless to anyone seeking to breach the system for user information. In addition, the customer's driver's license number, issuing authority number, and birthdate are stored in an encrypted vault. This safeguard is built into the system to verify a purchaser's age, not who they are, should law enforcement require such a verification. This vault is entirely separate from the database used to facilitate transactions at the retail point-of-sale.

Importantly, the system is built to identify age, not identity. Law enforcement could have access to the information in the vault following an appropriate legal process, but that would be the only access to that information as it would not be connected to the transactions at the time of the sale. This process is only available under subpoena and requires the cooperation of the government issuer.

The system does provide the ability to keep information on the number of purchases in order to comply with local laws that set maximum purchases of a product over a period of time. But, this too is done with an anonymous token and age. Personally identifiable information is not tracked across purchases when these limitations are put in place.

When using TruAge™, all personally identifiable information is eliminated from the transaction. Data breaches involve hacking into one database that contains personally identifiable information. Under this system, two separate databases would need to be compromised, *plus* randomly-generated tokens would need to be decrypted, *plus* a government database would need to be breeched to compromise a person's identity.

This program has been designed to comply with the most stringent existing and emerging consumer privacy regulations such as the General Data Protection Regulation (GDPR), which regulates data protection and privacy in the EU, and the California Consumer Privacy Act. The purpose of this program is to minimize capture of personally identifiable information from the more than 30 distinct pieces of information that exist on every driver's license to simply sell an age-restricted product. The only information accessed answers these three questions: 1) Is this a valid ID, 2) Does the customer look like the ID photo, and 3) Is the customer of legal age to purchase the age-restricted product. The way this system is designed can be a model for other use cases requiring different types of identity verification.

Status of the Program

TruAge™ is already being used and is demonstrating its success. It has been used in several stores in West Virginia as an initial test and it has proven its interoperability with the new digital Permanent Residence Card being developed by DHS/UCIS. There will be pilots conducted at stores in Texas in the third quarter of this year with a wider launch of the program in the fourth quarter. The goal is for TruAge™ to be universally accepted at all physical and online retailers nationwide where age-restricted products are sold. That will make the program more effective and more convenient for consumers.

* * *

The bottom line is that we have the technology to verify identity and protect privacy in the digital age. The convenience industry is at the forefront of doing that in the retail market for age-restricted purchases, but that system can serve as a model for other verification purposes and contexts. We look forward to working with the Committee as it continues to examine these important questions.

Sincerely,

Doug Kantor
NACS General Counsel

Chapter 2

Promoting Digital Privacy Technologies Act*

The Committee on Science, Space, and Technology

The Committee on Science, Space, and Technology, to whom was referred the bill (H.R. 847) to support research on privacy enhancing technologies and promote responsible data use, and for other purposes, having considered the same, reports favorably thereon with an amendment and recommends that the bill as amended do pass.

I. Amendment

The amendment is as follows:
   Strike all after the enacting clause and insert the following:

   SECTION 1. SHORT TITLE.
   This Act may be cited as the "Promoting Digital Privacy Technologies Act."
   SEC. 2. DEFINITION OF PRIVACY ENHANCING TECHNOLOGY.
   In this Act, the term "privacy enhancing technology"—
   (1) means any software or hardware solution, technical process, or other technological means of mitigating individuals' privacy risks arising from data processing by enhancing predictability, manageability, disassociability, and confidentiality; and
      (2) may include—

---

* This is an edited, reformatted and augmented version of House of Representatives Report 117–305, dated May 3, 2022.

In: Digital Identification
Editor: Lottie Gould
ISBN: 979-8-89113-494-2
© 2024 Nova Science Publishers, Inc.

(A) cryptographic techniques for facilitating computation or analysis on data while mitigating privacy risks;

(B) techniques for publicly sharing data without enabling inferences to be made about specific individuals;

(C) techniques for giving individuals' control over the dissemination, sharing, and use of their data;

(D) techniques for generating synthetic data; and

(E) any other technology or approach that reduces the risk of reidentification, including when combined with other information.

SEC. 3. NATIONAL SCIENCE FOUNDATION SUPPORT OF RESEARCH ON PRIVACY ENHANCING TECHNOLOGY.

The Director of the National Science Foundation, in consultation with other relevant Federal agencies (as determined by the Director), shall support merit-reviewed and competitively awarded research on privacy enhancing technologies, which may include—

(1) fundamental research on technologies for deidentification, pseudonymization, anonymization, or obfuscation to mitigate individuals' privacy risks in data sets while maintaining fairness, accuracy, and efficiency;

(2) fundamental research on algorithms and other similar mathematical tools used to protect individual privacy when collecting, storing, sharing, analyzing, or aggregating data;

(3) fundamental research on technologies that promote data minimization in data collection, sharing, and analytics that takes into account the trade-offs between the data minimization goals and the informational goals of data collection;

(4) research awards on privacy enhancing technologies coordinated with other relevant Federal agencies and programs;

(5) supporting education and workforce training research and development activities, including re-training and upskilling of the existing workforce, to grow the number of privacy enhancing technology researchers and practitioners;

(6) multidisciplinary socio-technical research that fosters broader understanding of privacy preferences, requirements, and human behavior to inform the design and adoption of effective privacy solutions;

(7) development of freely available privacy enhancing technology software libraries, platforms, and applications; and

(8) fundamental research on techniques that may undermine the protections provided by privacy enhancing technologies, the limitations of the

protections provided by privacy enhancing technologies, and the trade-offs between privacy and utility required for their deployment.

SEC. 4. INTEGRATION INTO THE COMPUTER AND NETWORK SECURITY PROGRAM.

Subparagraph (D) of section 4(a)(1) of the Cyber Security Research and Development Act (15 U.S.C. 7403(a)(1)(D)) is amended to read as follows:

"(D) privacy and confidentiality, including privacy enhancing technologies;".

SEC. 5. COORDINATION WITH THE NATIONAL INSTITUTE OF STANDARDS AND TECHNOLOGY AND OTHER STAKEHOLDERS.

(a) IN GENERAL.—The Director of the Office of Science and Technology Policy, acting through the Networking and Information Technology Research and Development Program, shall coordinate with the Director of the National Science Foundation, the Director of the National Institute of Standards and Technology, the Federal Trade Commission, and the heads of other Federal agencies, as appropriate, to accelerate the development, deployment, and adoption of privacy enhancing technologies.

(b) OUTREACH.—The Director of the National Institute of Standards and Technology shall conduct outreach to—

(1) receive input from private, public, and academic stakeholders on the development of privacy enhancing technologies; and

(2) facilitate and support ongoing public and private sector engagement to inform the development and dissemination of voluntary, consensus-based technical standards, guidelines, methodologies, procedures, and processes to cost-effectively increase the integration of privacy enhancing technologies in data collection, sharing, and analytics performed by the public and private sectors.

SEC. 6. REPORT ON PRIVACY ENHANCING TECHNOLOGY RESEARCH.

Not later than 3 years after the date of enactment of this Act, the Director of the Office of Science and Technology Policy, acting through the Networking and Information Technology Research and Development Program, shall, in coordination with the Director of the National Science Foundation, the Director of the National Institute of Standards and Technology, and the heads of other Federal agencies, as appropriate, submit to the Committee on Commerce, Science, and Transportation of the Senate, the Subcommittee on Commerce, Justice, Science, and Related Agencies of the Committee on Appropriations of the Senate, the Committee on Science,

Space, and Technology of the House of Representatives, and the Subcommittee on Commerce, Justice, Science, and Related Agencies of the Committee on Appropriations of the House of Representatives, a report containing—

(1) the progress of research on privacy enhancing technologies;

(2) the progress of the development of voluntary resources described under section 5(b)(2); and

(3) any policy recommendations that could facilitate and improve communication and coordination between the private sector and relevant Federal agencies for the implementation and adoption of privacy enhancing technologies.

SEC. 7. PROTECTING PERSONAL IDENTIFYING INFORMATION.

Any personal identifying information collected or stored through the activities authorized in this Act shall be done in accordance with section 690 of title 45, Code of Federal Regulations (relating to the protection of human subjects), or any successor regulation.

II. Purpose of the Bill

The purpose of the H.R. 847, the Promoting Digital Privacy Technologies Act, is to support research on privacy enhancing technologies and promote responsible data use.

III. Background and Need for the Legislation

Data about individuals is being generated at an increasing rate as more services rely on advertising to operate, and more devices are connected to the Internet. While Congress has not passed a general data protection law to promote the responsible use of this data, a number of U.S. states and other countries have started creating privacy laws that implicate organizations of all types and sizes. As a result, organizations are increasingly looking for low-cost and effective technologies and techniques to help them preserve the privacy of their consumers and employees. Privacy enhancing technologies (PETs), such as differential privacy and secure multiparty computation, have the potential to strengthen consumer privacy while still enabling the use of consumer data. PETs may also help with the implementation of other laws that encourage research activities that use large amounts of data, such as the National Artificial Intelligence Initiative Act (P.L. 116–283) and the Digital Accountability and Transparency Act (P.L. 113–101). However, the application of modern PETs is limited. Additional research and standard setting activities are necessary to broaden the applicability of the technology and encourage its further development and adoption. In addition, barriers remain to the successful coordination, development, and adoption of PETs by Federal agencies, especially for public health research.

The National Science Foundation (NSF) and the National Institute of Standards and Technology (NIST) are key agencies for privacy research and standards development. NSF has a long history of funding fundamental research and education activities related to privacy technologies. Similarly, NIST has long carried out research on privacy to inform the development and standardization of technologies that access personal data. For example, NIST created privacy standards for Federal systems in response to the Privacy Act of 1974 (P.L. 93–579). In 2020, NIST released the NIST Privacy Framework to help organizations identify and manage their privacy risks.

IV. Committee Hearings

Pursuant to House rule XIII, clause 3(c)(6), the Committee designates the following hearings as having been used to develop or consider the legislation:

On March 11, 2020, the Subcommittee on Research and Technology held a hearing entitled, "Reauthorization of the National Institute of Standards and Technology." The hearing included discussion of major areas of research under the National Institute of Standards and Technology laboratory programs, the agency's role in working with industry to advance U.S. competitiveness through standards development, and specifically NIST's work on a Privacy Framework. The Honorable Walter G. Copan, Undersecretary of Commerce for Standards and Technology and Director for the National Institute of Standards and Technology, testified before the committee.

On Wednesday, April 28, 2021, the Subcommittee on Research and Technology held a hearing held a hearing entitled, "National Science Foundation: Advancing Research for The Future of U.S. Innovation." The hearing included discussion of opportunities and challenges for leveraging and expanding the National Science Foundation mission to continue to advance excellent research; accelerating research to address major societal challenges;

and specifically a proposal for NSF to create a secure national data service. The hearing witnesses included Dr. Sethuraman Panchanathan, Director of the National Science Foundation, and Dr. Ellen Ochoa, Chair of the National Science Board.

On September 28, 2021, the Investigations and Oversight Subcommittee held a hearing entitled, "The Disinformation Black Box: Researching Social Media Data." The hearing included discussion of how researchers are able to access and analyze data from social media companies. Researchers testified about their work looking into the spread of misinformation and disinformation on social media platforms and how platforms drive traffic to advertisements and promoted posts. The hearing also explored the limitations of current tools, techniques, and datasets for researching social media platforms and how researchers have utilized information available to advertisers to flag privacy concerns to the platforms. The hearing examined how the Federal government can contribute to the ethical study of social media's impact on society while protecting the privacy of users. The hearing witnesses included Dr. Alan Mislove, Professor and Interim Dean of Khoury College of Computer Sciences at Northeastern University; Ms. Laura Edelson, Ph.D. Candidate and Co-Director of Cybersecurity for Democracy at New York University; and Dr. Kevin Leicht, Professor at the University of Illinois Urbana-Champaign Department of Sociology.

V. Committee Consideration and Votes

On January 19, 2022, the Full Committee on Science, Space, and Technology met to consider H.R. 847. Ms. Stevens offered an amendment in the nature of a substitute to make technical changes throughout the bill and update provisions in response to stakeholder feedback and Committee Member priorities, including expanding research provisions and ensuring OSTP coordinates PET research activities broadly across the Federal government. The amendment was agreed to on a voice vote. Ms. Stevens offered an amendment to make technical changes to the bill in response to agency technical assistance, including updating the definitions in the bill. The amendment was agreed to on a voice vote. Mr. Posey offered an amendment to ensure any personally identifiable information collected or stored through the activities in the Act would follow human subject data protections. The amendment was agreed to on a voice vote.

VI. Summary of Major Provisions of the Bill

Directs NSF to support competitive research on PETs, including through integration into research programs supported by the Directorate for Computer and Information Science and Engineering. Directs OSTP, in collaboration with other relevant Federal agencies, to accelerate the development, deployment and adoption of PETs. Directs NIST to conduct outreach to promote development of PETs. Requires a report to Congress 2 years after enactment.

VII. Section-by-Section Analysis (by Title and Section)

Sec. 1. Short title; Table of Contents Sec. 2. Definitions
   Sec. 3. National Science Foundation support of research on privacy enhancing technology
   Directs the NSF to support competitive, fundamental research on privacy enhancing technologies.
   Sec. 4. Integration into the computer and network security program
   Adds privacy enhancing technologies to a list of research areas supported by the NSF Directorate for Computer and Information Science and Engineering.
   Sec. 5. Coordination with the National Institute of Standards and Technology and other stakeholders
   Directs OSTP to coordinate activities related to privacy enhancing technologies between NSF, NIST, and the FTC. Directs NIST to conduct outreach and disseminate voluntary, consensus-based resources to facilitate the development of privacy enhancing technologies.
   Sec. 6. Report on research and standards development
   Directs OSTP to submit a report to Congress after 2 years that tracks the progress of privacy enhancing technology development and resources developed under Section 5, as well as makes recommendations to improve the coordination between Federal agencies and the private sector on privacy enhancing technologies.

VIII. Committee Views

Interagency Coordination—The Committee encourages NIST to coordinate its outreach activities with other Federal agencies that conduct activities related to privacy enhancing technologies, including the National Institutes of Health, the Centers for Disease Control, and the intelligence community.

IX. Cost Estimate

Pursuant to clause 3(c)(2) of rule XIII of the Rules of the House of Representatives, the Committee adopts as its own the estimate of new budget authority, entitlement authority, or tax expenditures or revenues contained in the cost estimate prepared by the Director of the Congressional Budget Office pursuant to section 402 of the Congressional Budget Act of 1974.

X. Congressional Budget Office Cost Estimate

U.S. Congress, Congressional Budget Office,
Washington, DC, April 20, 2022.
Hon. EDDIE BERNICE JOHNSON,

Chairwoman, Committee on Science, Space, and Technology, House of Representatives, Washington, DC.

DEAR MADAM CHAIRWOMAN: The Congressional Budget Office has prepared the enclosed cost estimate for H.R. 847, the Promoting Digital Privacy Technologies Act.

If you wish further details on this estimate, we will be pleased to provide them. The CBO staff contact is Janani Shankaran.

Sincerely,
Phillip L. Swagel,
Director.

Enclosure.

H.R. 847, Promoting Digital Privacy Technologies Act As ordered reported by the House Committee on Science, Space, and Technology on January 19, 2022			
By Fiscal Year, Millions of Dollars	2022	2022-2026	2022-2031
Direct Spending (Outlays)	0	0	0
Revenues	0	0	0
Increase or Decrease (-) in the Deficit	0	0	0
Spending Subject to Appropriation (Outlays)	*	2	not estimated
Statutory pay-as-you-go procedures apply?	No	Mandate Effects	
Increases on-budget deficits in any of the four consecutive 10-year periods beginning in 2032?	No	Contains intergovernmental mandate?	No
		Contains private-sector mandate?	No
* = between zero and $500,000.			

H.R. 847 would direct the National Institute of Standards and Technology (NIST) to conduct outreach on privacy-enhancing technologies and would require the National Science Foundation (NSF) to support related research. The bill also would direct the Office of Science and Technology Policy to report to the Congress on research in privacy-enhancing technologies and related policy recommendations.

Based on the costs of similar activities, CBO estimates that NIST would need three employees at an average annual cost of $175,000 annually to conduct the outreach. In recent years, the NSF has awarded between $20 million and $40 million annually in grants to support research on privacy-enhancing technologies. On that basis, CBO estimates that any additional costs incurred by the NSF under H.R. 847 would not be significant. In addition, CBO estimates that cost of the required report would be insignificant. In total, CBO estimates that implementing H.R. 847 would cost $2 million over the 2022–2026 period; such spending would be subject to the availability of appropriated funds.

The CBO staff contacts for this estimate are Janani Shankaran and David Hughes. The estimate was reviewed by H. Samuel Papenfuss, Deputy Director of Budget Analysis.

XI. Federal Mandates Statement

H.R. 847 contains no unfunded mandates.

XII. Committee Oversight Findings and Recommendations

The Committee's oversight findings and recommendations are reflected in the body of this report.

XIII. Statement on General Performance Goals and Objectives

The goals and objectives of H.R. 847 are to authorize research and standards setting activities at the National Science Foundation (NSF) and the National Institute of Standards and Technology (NIST) for privacy enhancing technologies. The bill also promotes interagency coordination on privacy enhancing technologies.

XIV. Federal Advisory Committee Statement

H.R. 847 does not authorize an advisory committee.

XV. Duplication of Federal Programs

Pursuant to clause 3(c)(5) of rule XIII of the Rules of the House of Representatives, the Committee finds that no provision of H.R. 847 establishes or reauthorizes a program of the federal government known to be duplicative of another federal program, including any program that was included in a report to Congress pursuant to section 21 of Public Law 111–139 or the most recent Catalog of Federal Domestic Assistance.

XVI. Earmark Identification

Pursuant to clause 9(e), 9(f), and 9(g) of rule XXI, the Committee finds that H.R. 847 contains no earmarks, limited tax benefits, or limited tariff benefits.

XVII. Applicability to the Legislative Branch

The Committee finds that H.R. 847 does not relate to the terms and conditions of employment or access to public services or accommodations within the meaning of section 102(b)(3) of the Congressional Accountability Act (Public Law 104–1).

XVIII. Statement on Preemption of State, Local, or Tribal Law

This bill is not intended to preempt any state, local, or tribal law.

XIX. Changes in Existing Law Made by the Bill, as Reported

In compliance with clause 3(e) of rule XIII of the Rules of the House of Representatives, changes in existing law made by the bill, as reported, are shown as follows (existing law proposed to be omitted is enclosed in black brackets, new matter is printed in italics, and existing law in which no change is proposed is shown in roman):

Cyber Security Research and Development Act

SEC. 4. NATIONAL SCIENCE FOUNDATION RESEARCH.
    (a) COMPUTER AND NETWORK SECURITY RESEARCH GRANTS.—
        (1) IN GENERAL.—The Director shall award grants for basic research on innovative approaches to the structure of computer and network hardware and software that are aimed at enhancing computer security. Research areas may include—

(A) authentication, cryptography, and other secure data communications technology;
(B) computer forensics and intrusion detection;
(C) reliability of computer and network applications, middleware, operating systems, control systems, and communications infrastructure;
ø(D) privacy and confidentiality;¿
(D) privacy and confidentiality, including privacy enhancing technologies;
(E) network security architecture, including tools for security administration and analysis;
(F) emerging threats;
(G) vulnerability assessments and techniques for quantifying risk;
(H) remote access and wireless security;
(I) enhancement of law enforcement ability to detect, investigate, and prosecute cyber-crimes, including those that involve piracy of intellectual property;
(J) secure fundamental protocols that are integral to inter-network communications and data exchange;
(K) secure software engineering and software assurance, including—
(i) programming languages and systems that include fundamental security features;
(ii) portable or reusable code that remains secure when deployed in various environments;
(iii) verification and validation technologies to ensure that requirements and specifications have been implemented; and
(iv) models for comparison and metrics to assure that required standards have been met;
(L) holistic system security that—
(v) addresses the building of secure systems from trusted and untrusted components;
(vi) proactively reduces vulnerabilities;
(vii) addresses insider threats; and
(viii) supports privacy in conjunction with improved security;
(M) monitoring and detection;
(N) mitigation and rapid recovery methods;
(O) security of wireless networks and mobile devices;
(P) security of cloud infrastructure and services;
(Q) security of election-dedicated voting system software and hardware; and

(R) role of the human factor in cybersecurity and the interplay of computers and humans and the physical world.

(2) MERIT REVIEW; COMPETITION.—Grants shall be awarded under this section on a merit-reviewed competitive basis.

(3) AUTHORIZATION OF APPROPRIATIONS.—There are authorized to be appropriated to the National Science Foundation to carry out this subsection—

(A) $35,000,000 for fiscal year 2003;
(B) $40,000,000 for fiscal year 2004;
(C) $46,000,000 for fiscal year 2005;
(D) $52,000,000 for fiscal year 2006; and
(E) $60,000,000 for fiscal year 2007.

(b) COMPUTER AND NETWORK SECURITY RESEARCH CENTERS.—

(1) IN GENERAL.—The Director shall award multiyear grants, subject to the availability of appropriations, to institutions of higher education, nonprofit research institutions, or consortia thereof to establish multidisciplinary Centers for Computer and Network Security Research. Institutions of higher education, nonprofit research institutions, or consortia thereof receiving such grants may partner with 1 or more government laboratories or for-profit institutions, or other institutions of higher education or nonprofit research institutions.

(2) MERIT REVIEW; COMPETITION.—Grants shall be awarded under this subsection on a merit-reviewed competitive basis.

(3) PURPOSE.—The purpose of the Centers shall be to generate innovative approaches to computer and network security by conducting cutting-edge, multidisciplinary research in computer and network security, including improving the security and resiliency of information technology, reducing cyber vulnerabilities, and anticipating and mitigating consequences of cyber attacks on critical infrastructure, by conducting research in the areas described in subsection (a)(1).

(4) APPLICATIONS.—An institution of higher education, non-profit research institution, or consortia thereof seeking funding under this subsection shall submit an application to the Director at such time, in such manner, and containing such information as the Director may require. The application shall include, at a minimum, a description of—

(A) the research projects that will be undertaken by the Center and the contributions of each of the participating entities;

(B) how the Center will promote active collaboration among scientists and engineers from different disciplines, such as computer scientists, engineers, mathematicians, and social science researchers;

(C) how the Center will contribute to increasing the number and quality of computer and network security researchers and other professionals, including individuals from groups historically underrepresented in these fields; and

(D) how the Center will disseminate research results quickly and widely to improve cyber security in information technology networks, products, and services.

(5) CRITERIA.—In evaluating the applications submitted under paragraph (4), the Director shall consider, at a minimum—

(A) the ability of the applicant to generate innovative approaches to computer and network security and effectively carry out the research program;

(B) the experience of the applicant in conducting research on computer and network security and the capacity of the applicant to foster new multidisciplinary collaborations;

(C) the capacity of the applicant to attract and provide adequate support for a diverse group of undergraduate and graduate students and postdoctoral fellows to pursue computer and network security research;

(D) the extent to which the applicant will partner with government laboratories, for-profit entities, other institutions of higher education, or nonprofit research institutions, and the role the partners will play in the research undertaken by the Center;

(E) the demonstrated capability of the applicant to conduct high performance computation integral to complex computer and network security research, through on-site or off-site computing;

(F) the applicant's affiliation with private sector entities involved with industrial research described in subsection (a)(1);

(G) the capability of the applicant to conduct research in a secure environment;

(H) the applicant's affiliation with existing research programs of the Federal Government;

(I) the applicant's experience managing public-private partnerships to transition new technologies into a commercial setting or the government user community;

(J) the capability of the applicant to conduct interdisciplinary cybersecurity research, basic and applied, such as in law, economics, or behavioral sciences; and

(K) the capability of the applicant to conduct research in areas such as systems security, wireless security, networking and protocols, formal methods and networking and information technology, nanotechnology, or industrial control systems.

(6) ANNUAL MEETING.—The Director shall convene an annual meeting of the Centers in order to foster collaboration and communication between Center participants.

(7) AUTHORIZATION OF APPROPRIATIONS.—There are authorized to be appropriated for the National Science Foundation to carry out this subsection—
  (A) $12,000,000 for fiscal year 2003;
  (B) $24,000,000 for fiscal year 2004;
  (C) $36,000,000 for fiscal year 2005;
  (D) $36,000,000 for fiscal year 2006; and
  (E) $36,000,000 for fiscal year 2007.

Chairwoman Eddie Bernice Johnson (D-TX)

Full Committee Markup of:
  H.R. 4521, the "Bioeconomy Research and Development Act of 2021"
  H.R. 847, the "Promoting Digital Privacy Technologies Act"
  H.R. 4270, the "Abandoned Well Remediation Research and Development Act"
  H.R. 4819, the "National Nuclear University Research Infrastructure Reinvestment Act of 2021"
  H.R. 6291, the "Microelectronics Research for Energy Innovation Act" or "Micro Act" January 19, 2022

Welcome to the first Science Committee markup of 2022. Today we are marking up five good bipartisan bills.

The first bill to be considered is the Bioeconomy Research and Development Act. I first want to thank Ranking Member Lucas for partnering with me on this bill. This legislation creates a national engineering biology initiative in support of U.S. leadership in the 21st Century Bioeconomy.

Advances in engineering biology will drive innovation across nearly all sectors of our economy. Europe and China long ago took steps to implement a bioeconomy strategy. Our own efforts have progressed in fits and starts. The time to implement a coherent national strategy is now. I'll speak more about this bill when we call it up.

The next item we will take up today is the Promoting Digital Privacy Technologies Act. I want to thank Representatives Stevens and Gonzalez for their thoughtful work on this legislation.

Privacy enhancing technologies have the potential to vastly improve the way we protect peoples' privacy when processing information about them. This bill seeks to accelerate the development of these technologies. It would fund research into privacy enhancing technologies at the National Science Foundation. It would also authorize outreach and standard-setting activities at the National Institute of Standards and Technology. Finally, the bill promotes coordination on the development of these technologies across the Federal government. Getting privacy right in a way that allows for the effective use of information is a difficult challenge. This bill will promote new avenues of research to strike that balance.

I am happy to be an original cosponsor, along with Ranking Member Lucas, on the next bill we are marking up: the Abandoned Well Remediation Research and Development Act, introduced by Mr. Lamb and Ms. Bice. This bipartisan bill creates a research, development, and demonstration program at the Department of Energy to tackle the ever-growing problem of abandoned oil and gas wells in the U.S. It would increase the efficiency of remediation, mitigate environmental harms, and reduce methane emissions. It would also improve technologies to enable the widespread mapping of unrecorded abandoned wells around the country, some of which can date back as far as the 1850s. As we transition to a clean energy economy, it is critical that we have sound and proven technologies to mitigate the harmful methane emissions of hundreds of thousands, if not millions of abandoned wells in our communities.

The next bill we will consider is the National Nuclear University Research Infrastructure Reinvestment Act of 2021, introduced by Representatives Gonzalez, Foster, Casten, and Meijer. This bill builds off historic nuclear energy research and development legislation enacted into law as part of the Energy Act of 2020.

The bill has two major thrusts – first, to ensure existing nuclear energy university infrastructure is well-maintained and potentially upgraded; and second, to build new nuclear science and engineering university facilities. And the bill also places strong emphasis on ensuring all activities include a wide variety of participants beyond those who already have established nuclear science capabilities, including historically Black colleges and universities, Tribal colleges or universities, and other minority-serving institutions.

Finally, the last bill we will consider to today is the Microelectronics Research for Energy Innovation Act, which was sponsored by Representatives Tonko and Ellzey. This legislation seeks to leverage the unique capabilities and technical expertise of the Department of Energy to accelerate transformational advancements in the field of microelectronics, which play an increasingly significant role in our daily lives, and which are essential to maintaining U.S. national security and global economic and scientific leadership. Specifically, this bill would direct the Secretary of Energy to carry out a crosscutting initiative in microelectronics, including research activities aimed at driving progress in related scientific fields as well as large-scale, center-based efforts focused on addressing specific challenges. The bill also includes an emphasis on workforce development, education, and outreach to ensure that we are engaging students of all ages in this exciting field and laying the groundwork for the microelectronics workforce of the future. I urge my colleagues to support this important legislation.

Finally, I want to address a topic that came up very late in the process. Groups approached us yesterday afternoon asking to add in Davis Bacon prevailing wage requirements to three of the bills we are marking up today. This was much too late in the process to try and deal with this issue. While I am a supporter of Davis Bacon, some of my friends on the other side of the aisle are not. Trying to address this issue while maintaining strong bipartisan support is something that simply could not be done in a hasty fashion.

I know the gentleman from New Jersey is a strong advocate for Davis Bacon, and I would like to try and find a path forward on this issue as we move forward. However, I don't want to sugar coat how difficult addressing this issue will be while maintaining bipartisan support for the legislation.

Chairwoman JOHNSON. Now, I will recognize our Ranking Member, Mr. Lucas, for his opening remarks.

Opening Statement of Ranking Member Frank Lucas

Full Committee Markup of H.R. 4521, H.R. 847, H.R. 4270, H.R. 4819, and H.R. 6291
January 19, 2022

Thank you, Chairwoman Johnson for holding today's markup. This morning we will consider 5 bipartisan bills.

The first, the "Bioeconomy Research and Development Act of 2021", is a bill I was proud to sponsor with the Chairwoman. I will discuss this legislation further when the Chair brings it up for debate and I offer an amendment.

The second bill is H.R. 847, the "Promoting Digital Privacy Technologies Act." This legislation supports research activities to advance innovative technologies to safeguard individuals' privacy. As advanced technologies like AI begin accessing and analyzing large data sets, it will be critical we have technologies to ensure people's personally identifiable information is protected.

The legislation also directs NIST to work with stakeholders to develop voluntary consensus standards for incorporating these technologies into federal and commercial applications. I want to thank Chairwoman Stevens and Representative Gonzalez for leading this important legislation. I encourage my colleagues to support the bill.

The third bill is H.R. 4270, the "Abandoned Well Remediation Research and Development Act." This legislation authorizes DOE to conduct research on issues surrounding abandoned wells. The bill will allow us improve data on the location of abandoned wells; identify better processes for plugging, reclaiming, and repurposing wells; and help us mitigate the potential environmental impacts of leaking wells.

This is a major issue for Oklahoma and my district. Drive across the state and you'll see countless wells sitting on top of some of the nation's largest gas and oil fields. This bill will help give producers, landowners, and state and local governments the tools they need to manage these wells. I applaud my fellow Oklahoman, Rep. Stephanie Bice, for working with Rep. Lamb on this important bipartisan legislation.

The fourth bill we will consider is H.R. 4819, the "National Nuclear University Research Infrastructure Reinvestment Act of 2021." The bill, authored by Rep. Anthony Gonzalez, builds off the improvements to the Nuclear Energy University Program included in the Energy Act of 2020. It will establish up to 4 new university-based research reactors, which would be able to collaborate and help the Advanced Reactor Demonstration Program and the Low-Dose Radiation Program.

I thank Rep. Gonzalez and Rep. Foster for working together on this bipartisan bill to advance our nation's nuclear energy capabilities. Nuclear energy is critical to our nation's energy security and independence. This bill will help ensure we our developing the workforce and advanced reactors of the future to make this a reality.

Finally, we will consider H.R. 6291, the "Microelectronics Research for Energy Innovation Act" or the "Micro Act." The bill directs DOE to carry out a cross-cutting research, development, and demonstration program on microelectronics to accelerate U.S. global competitiveness in this critical technology area.

DOE possesses unique technical expertise and research infrastructure that can drive the development of the next generation of microelectronics. The Department and its world-leading national laboratory system must play a significant role in our federal strategy to shore up our international competitiveness in the microelectronics field and confront related national security threats.

The legislation complements the CHIPS Act, signed into law last year, to address the decline of domestic semiconductor manufacturing and promote advanced semiconductor development in the United States. The Micro Act will help ensure DOE's critical participation in this work and should be considered alongside the DOE Science for the Future Act as an essential component of a U.S. competitiveness legislative package. I thank Rep. Tonko and Rep. Ellzey for working on this important bipartisan legislation.

Each of these bills harnesses America's incredible scientific and technological prowess to address pressing challenges and improve our future. This is a great example of what the Science Committee can do when we work together.

I want to thank Chairwoman Johnson and her staff for working collaboratively on getting these bills ready for markup, and for working through the amendments we will consider today. I have every expectation this will be a productive and collegial markup.

I yield back.

H. R. 847

To support research on privacy enhancing technologies and promote responsible data use, and for other purposes.

IN THE HOUSE OF REPRESENTATIVES
FEBRUARY 4, 2021

Ms. STEVENS (for herself and Mr. GONZALEZ of Ohio) introduced the following bill; which was referred to the Committee on Science, Space, and Technology

A BILL

To support research on privacy enhancing technologies and promote responsible data use, and for other purposes.

1 Be it enacted by the Senate and House of Representa-
2 tives of the United States of America in Congress assembled,
3 SECTION 1. SHORT TITLE.
4 This Act may be cited as the "Promoting Digital Pri-
5 vacy Technologies Act".
6 SEC. 2. DEFINITIONS.
7 In this Act:

(1) PERSONAL DATA.—The term "personal data" means information that identifies, is linked to, or is reasonably linkable to, an individual or a consumer device, including derived data.

(2) PRIVACY ENHANCING TECHNOLOGY.—The term "privacy enhancing technology"—

A) means any software solution, technical processes, or other technological means of enhancing the privacy and confidentiality of an individual's personal data in data or sets of data; and

B) Includes anonymization and pseudonymization techniques, filtering tools, anti-tracking technology, differential privacy tools, synthetic data, and secure multi-party computation.

Sec. 3. National Science Foundation Support of Research on Privacy Enhancing Technology

The Director of the National Science Foundation, in consultation with other relevant Federal agencies (as determined by the Director), shall support merit-reviewed and competitively awarded research on privacy enhancing technologies, which may include—

(1) research on technologies for deidentification, pseudonymization, anonymization, or obfuscation of personal data in data sets while maintaining fairness, accuracy, and efficiency;
(2) fundamental research on algorithms and other similar mathematical tools used to protect individual privacy when collecting, storing, sharing, or aggregating data;
(3) fundamental research on technologies that promote data minimization principles in data collection, sharing, and analytics; and
(4) research awards on privacy enhancing technologies coordinated with other relevant Federal agencies and programs.

Sec. 4. Integration into the Computer and Network Security Program

Subparagraph (D) of section 4(a)(1) of the Cyber Security Research and Development Act (15 U.S.C. 7403(a)(1)(D)) is amended to read as follows:

"(D) privacy enhancing technologies and confidentiality;"

Sec. 5. Coordination with the National Institute of Standards and Technology and Other Stakeholders

(a) IN GENERAL.—The Director of the Office of Science and Technology Policy, acting through the Networking and Information Technology Research and Devel opment Program, shall coordinate with the Director of the National Science Foundation, the Director of the National Institute of Standards and Technology, and the Federal Trade Commission to accelerate the development and use of privacy enhancing technologies.

(b) OUTREACH.—The Director of the National Institute of Standards and Technology shall conduct outreach to—
   1) receive input from private, public, and academic stakeholders, including the National Institutes of Health and the Centers for Disease Control and Prevention, for the purpose of facilitating public health research, on the development of privacy enhancing technologies; and

2) develop ongoing public and private sector engagement to create and disseminate voluntary, consensus-based resources to increase the integration of privacy enhancing technologies in data collection, sharing, and analytics by the public and private sectors.

Sec. 6. Report on Research and Standards Development

Not later than 2 years after the date of enactment of this Act, the Director of the Office of Science and Technology Policy, acting through the Networking and Information Technology Research and Development Program, shall, in coordination with the Director of the National Science Foundation and the Director of the National Institute of Standards and Technology, submit to the Committee on Commerce, Science, and Transportation of the Senate, the Subcommittee on Commerce, Justice, Science, and Related Agencies of the Committee on Appropriations of the Senate, the Committee on Science, Space, and Technology of the House of Representatives, and the Subcommittee on Commerce, Justice, Science, and Related Agencies of the Committee on Appropriations of the House of Representatives, a report containing—

(1) the progress of research on privacy enhancing technologies;
(2) the progress of the development of voluntary resources described under section 5(b)(2); and
(3) any policy recommendations of the Directors that could facilitate and improve communication and coordination between the private sector, the National Science Foundation, and relevant Federal agencies through the implementation of privacy enhancing technologies.

We will now consider H.R. 847, the *Promoting Digital Privacy Technologies Act*. The Clerk will report the bill.

The CLERK. H.R. 847, to support research on privacy, enhancing technologies, and promote responsible data use and for other purposes.

[The bill follows:]

Chairwoman JOHNSON. Without objection, the bill is considered as read and open to amendment at any point.
  Does anyone wish to be recognized to speak on this underlying bill?
  Ms. STEVENS. Madam Speaker, I wish to be recognized. Madam Chair.
  Chairwoman JOHNSON. Ms. Stevens—yes, you're recognized for 5 minutes.
  Ms. STEVENS. Thank you, Madam Chair. I'm pleased to offer this amendment, this bipartisan amendment in the nature of a substitute for H.R. 847, the *Promoting Digital Privacy Technologies Act*. I want to sincerely thank my colleagues, Representative Gonzalez from Ohio, as well as Senators Catherine Cortez Masto and Senator Deb Fischer, for working with me to introduce this legislation last year.
  Americans are online. Practically any digital action that internet users take from social media or shopping online to browsing news or using email creates data that is stored by companies or organizations. More and more data about each and every one of us is being generated faster and faster each day at a rate that history has never seen. In most States companies can use, share, or sell the data they collect. Since most of the data economy is invisible, Americans are not able to see this constant flow of their information.
  I believe we can safeguard our most sensitive information online without having to sacrifice innovation. Finding this balance requires us to explore how we can integrate the privacy-enhancing technologies to protect Americans' most sensitive data and also harness new innovation capabilities through these privacy-enhancing technologies.
  The *Promoting Digital Privacy Technologies Act* will support research, work force development, standard-setting, and government coordination for privacy-enhancing technologies, or PETs. PETs are a broad range of technologies that allow organizations to collect, share, and use data while mitigating the privacy risks that arise from those activities. Differential privacy, encryption, and secure multiparty computation are just some examples of these technologies. PETs are enabling technologies allowing for the improvement of critical industries of the future such as artificial intelligence and data science without privacy risks. The technologies also have the potential to enable broader use of Federal data sets as privacy risks are often the biggest barrier to open-government efforts.
  The amendment in the nature of a substitute to H.R. 847 will support the development, deployment, and adoption of PETs. It directs the National Science Foundation, a favorite of this Committee, to conduct fundamental privacy research that can help improve these technologies, assess their limitations, and broaden their capabilities. This amendment also directs NSF to support work force development activities in order to help address the growing shortage of privacy professionals and researchers across the United States of America.
  The amendment supports the activities of another favorite agency of this Committee, the National Institute of Standards and

Technology, to facilitate the development of standards and guidance with the integration of PETs into the public and private sectors.

And finally, this amendment will be directing the White House Office of Science and Technology Policy to coordinate Federal activities to accelerate the development, deployment, and adoption of PETs across the government.

Congress has been considering different proposals for privacy legislation for what seems like decades now. While many of those reforms fall outside the jurisdiction of this Committee, legislation like this that supports privacy research and standard-setting, utilizing and harnessing incredible technologies will help set and address some of the unmet needs.

So we are proud partners—I'm a proud partner of colleagues from across the chamber into the Senate and certainly across the aisle as we work together and to enhance privacy protections for our constituents. This is a phenomenal way to work with the private sector as they help to advise and inform the National Institute of Standards and Technology. This does not need to be seen as regulatory. In fact, it is collaborative and it is enhancing and progressing economies of scale while certainly protecting individual Americans.

So with that, I encourage all of you to support this amendment, and I will yield back.

Chairwoman JOHNSON. Thank you very much.

Does anyone else wish to be recognized at this point to speak on the underlying bill?

Mr. GONZALEZ. Madam Chair, I move to strike the last word.

Chairwoman JOHNSON. Mr. Gonzalez is recognized for 5 minutes.

Mr. GONZALEZ. Thank you, Chairwoman Johnson, for holding this morning's markup of H.R. 847, the *Promoting Digital Privacy Technologies Act*. I'd also like to thank my colleague Ms. Stevens for offering this amendment in the nature of a substitute, which makes important technical changes to the underlying bill, which we introduced nearly a year ago.

Advancements in the utilization of data are helping spur new innovations and advancements in our economy. Data analytics are helping manufacturers improve efficiencies, streamline processes, and cover insights that drive growth such as helping to predict equipment failure and conduct preventative maintenance, excuse me. Our healthcare providers are using—utilizing data to highlight trends and threats and create predictive models. For example, by using big data, researchers can identify disease genes and biomarkers to help patients pinpoint health issues they may face in the future. The results can allow healthcare organizations to design personalized treatments.

More recently, we've seen the use of data analytics to help manage the spread of COVID–19. While this revolution offers an opportunity to solve some of the world's most significant challenges, it certainly raises legitimate privacy questions and concerns about how to best protect our personal data. We must ensure these data analysis innovations do not put Americans' private information at risk.

That is why I was proud to join Chairwoman Stevens in introducing this legislation, which directs the National Science Foundation to support research on privacy-enhancing technologies that will mitigate privacy risks and ensure confidentiality. It also takes steps to improve how business and government integrate privacy-enhancing technologies into daily operations to better safeguard Americans' most sensitive information.

Again, I want to thank Ms. Stevens for working with me on this important legislation and many other things. We work very well together. I encourage my colleagues to support this amendment and this legislation, which takes important steps in ensuring responsible data usage and protecting an individual's privacy.

Thank you, and I yield back the balance of my time.

Mr. GONZALEZ. Chairwoman, you're muted.

Chairwoman JOHNSON. Sorry, I was muted. Anyone else seeking time on this amendment?

Ms. ROSS. Madam Chair, I move to strike the last word. This is Representative Ross.

Chairwoman JOHNSON. You're recognized.

Ms. ROSS. Thank you so much, Madam Chair and Ranking Member. And this is such an incredible bill and such an important issue for our markup today. I also want to thank the sponsors of the bill for bringing it forward.

H.R. 847, the *Promoting Digital Privacy Technologies Act,* authorizes research standards-setting activities at the NSF and NIST for privacy-enhancing technologies. Advancements in large-scale data analysis have led to innovations in the clean energy, healthcare, and manufacturing industries. However, Americans also have the right to privacy and the knowledge that their sensitive personal information is handled in ways consistent with their interests.

My district includes much of the Research Triangle, a major technology and innovation hub. It also includes NC (North Carolina) State University, a preeminent land-grant research institution. That's why I'm particularly pleased that this bill directs agencies to cooperate with public, private, and academic partners to produce consensus, privacy-enhancing standards. This will ensure that we strike the appropriate balance between protecting personal data and fostering the innovation that has made the United States a global technology leader.

I support the bill, and thank you, Madam Chair. I yield back.

Chairwoman JOHNSON. Well, thank you very much.

Now, we have already spoken on the first amendment on this roster, but I must ask Ms. Stevens if you want to be recognized again.

Ms. STEVENS. Yes, to introduce the amendment on the technical corrections, Madam Chair?

STAFF. First, we need to call up this amendment.

Chairwoman JOHNSON. Well, we haven't called up the amendment yet, but most of the statements have been on the substitute on the amendment, and so we're at a point where——

STAFF. You can just ask the Clerk to report the amendment.

Chairwoman JOHNSON. We can ask the Clerk to report the amendment at the desk and then close it out unless there are other statements.
Chairwoman JOHNSON. Would the Clerk report?
The CLERK. Amendment No. 1, amendment in the nature of a substitute to H.R. 847 offered by Ms. Stevens of Michigan.
[The amendment of Ms. Stevens follows:]

Amendment in the Nature of a Substitute to H.R. 847 Offered by Ms. Stevens of Michigan

Strike all after the enacting clause and insert the following:

Section 1. Short Title

This Act may be cited as the "Promoting Digital Privacy Technologies Act."

SEC. 2. Definitions

In this Act:

1) PERSONALDATA.—The term "personal data" means information that identifies, is linked to, or is reasonably linkable to, an individual or a consumer device, including derived data that can be used to identify an individual or consumer device.
2) PRIVACY ENHANCING TECHNOLOGY.—The term "privacy enhancing technology"—
    A. means any software solution, technical processes, or other technological means of enhancing the privacy and confidentiality of an individual's personal data in data or sets of data; and
    B. may include—
        (i) techniques for facilitating computation or analysis on personal data while maintaining the confidentiality of that data;
        (ii) techniques for safeguarding personal data contained within large datasets;
        (iii) techniques for giving individuals' control over the dissemination and use of personal data;

(iv) techniques for generating synthetic data; and
(v) any other technology or approach that reduces the risk of re-identification, including when combined with other information, to provide for reasonable privacy and confidentiality protections.

Sec. 3. National Science Foundation Support of ReSearch on Privacy Enhancing TechNology

The Director of the National Science Foundation, in consultation with other relevant Federal agencies (as determined by the Director), shall support merit-reviewed and competitively awarded research on privacy enhancing technologies, which may include—

(1) fundamental research on technologies for de-identification, pseudonymization, anonymization, or obfuscation of personal data in data sets while maintaining fairness, accuracy, and efficiency;
(2) fundamental research on algorithms and other similar mathematical tools used to protect individual privacy when collecting, storing, sharing, or aggregating data;
(3) fundamental research on technologies that promote data minimization in data collection, sharing, and analytics that takes into account the trade-offs between the data minimization goals and the informational goals of data collection;
(4) research awards on privacy enhancing technologies coordinated with other relevant Federal agencies and programs;
(5) supporting education and workforce training research and development activities, including retraining and upskilling of the existing workforce, to grow the number of privacy enhancing technology researchers and practitioners;
(6) development of freely available privacy enhancing technology software libraries, platforms, and applications; and
(7) fundamental research on techniques that may undermine the protections provided by privacy enhancing technologies, the limitations of the protections provided by privacy enhancing technologies, and the trade-offs between privacy and utility required for their deployment.

Sec. 4. Integration into the Computer And Network Security Program

Subparagraph (D) of section 4(a)(1) of the Cyber Security Research and Development Act (15U.S.C.7403(a)(1)(D)) is amended to read as follows:

"(D) privacy and confidentiality, including privacy enhancing technologies;"

Sec. 5. Coordination with the National Institute of Standards and Echnology and Other Stakeholders

a. IN GENERAL.—The Director of the Office of Science and Technology Policy, acting through the Networking and Information Technology Research and Development Program, shall coordinate with the Director of the National Science Foundation, the Director of the National Institute of Standards and Technology, the Federal Trade Commission, and the heads of other Federal agencies, as appropriate, to accelerate the development, deployment, and adoption of privacy enhancing technologies.
b. OUTREACH.—The Director of the National Institute of Standards and Technology shall conduct outreach to—
   (1) receive input from private, public, and academic stakeholders on the development of privacy enhancing technologies; and
   (2) facilitate and support ongoing public and private sector engagement to create and disseminate voluntary, consensus-based technical standards, best practices, guidelines, methodologies, procedures, and processes to cost-effectively ensure the integration of privacy enhancing technologies in data collection, sharing, and analytics performed by the public and private sectors.

Sec. 6. Report on Privacy Enhancing Technology Research

Not later than 3 years after the date of enactment of this Act, the Director of the Office of Science and Technology Policy, acting through the Networking and Information Technology Research and Development Program, shall, in coordination with the Director of the National Science Foundation, the Director of the National Institute of Standards and Technology, and the heads of other Federal agencies, as appropriate, submit to the Committee on Commerce, Science, and Transportation of the Senate, the Subcommittee on Commerce, Justice, Science, and Related Agencies of the Committee on Appropriations of the Senate, the Committee on Science, Space, and Technology of the House of Representatives, and the Subcommittee on Commerce, Justice, Science, and Related Agencies of the Committee on Appropriations of the House of Representatives, a report containing—

1) the progress of research on privacy enhancing technologies;
2) the progress of the development of voluntary resources described under section 5(b)(2); and
3) any policy recommendations that could facilitate and improve communication and coordination between the private sector and relevant Federal agencies for the implementation of privacy enhancing technologies.

Chairwoman JOHNSON. Thank you. Ms. Stevens, in your opening remarks you also spoke to this amendment. Would you like to speak again or shall we just ask if there are other comments?

Ms. STEVENS. I will move to speak again.

Chairwoman JOHNSON. You're recognized.

Ms. STEVENS. In part, this amendment, Madam Chair, does include technical corrections and language that incorporates feedback from our friends at the National Science Foundation and the National Institute of Standards and Technology. Specifically when writing legislation that may impact the privacy of our constituents, the American people, it is important to get our terms and definitions right.

The amendment updates the definition of privacy-enhancing technologies and the underlying——

Chairwoman JOHNSON. Ms. Stevens?

Ms. STEVENS. Yes?

Chairwoman JOHNSON. You're speaking to the next amendment.

Ms. STEVENS. Yes.

Chairwoman JOHNSON. We're going to close out——

Ms. STEVENS. OK. We'll close out that.

Chairwoman JOHNSON. OK.

Ms. STEVENS. One more movement, it's been a joy to work with Mr. Gonzalez, and we're very glad to have comments from Ms. Ross on the record. Thank you.

STAFF. OK.

Ms. STEVENS. It's an overzealous morning.

Chairwoman JOHNSON. Yes. If there are no additional comments, we will move to this next amendment and vote on the substitute amendment later.

The next amendment on the roster is an amendment offered by the gentlelady from Michigan, Ms. Stevens, and she's recognized to report the—to speak on the amendment. You have an amendment at the desk, and the Clerk will report the amendment.

The CLERK. Amendment No. 2, amendment to the amendment in the nature of a substitute to H.R. 847 offered by Ms. Stevens of Michigan.

[The amendment of Ms. Stevens follows:]

Amendment to the Amendment in the Nature of a Substitute tto H.R. 847 Offered by Ms. Stevens of Michigan

Page 1, strike lines 4 through 12 and insert the following:

Sec. 2. Definition of Privacy Enhancing Technology

In this Act, the term "privacy enhancing technology"—

Page 1, lines 13 through 17, strike "means any software solution, technical processes, or other technological means of enhancing the privacy and confidentiality of an individual's personal data in data or sets of data;" and insert "means any software or hardware solution, technical process, or other technological means of mitigating individuals' privacy risks arising from data processing by enhancing predictability, manageability, disassociability, and confidentiality;"

Page 2, lines 1 through 4, amend clause (i) to read as follows:

(i) cryptographic techniques for facilitating computation or analysis on data while mitigating privacy risks;

Page 2, lines 5 and 6, amend clause (ii) to read as follows:

(ii) techniques for publicly sharing data without enabling inferences to be made about specific individuals;

Page 2, line 8, insert, "sharing," after "dissemination."

Page 2, line 9, strike "personal" and insert "their."

Page 2, lines 15 and 16, strike, "to provide for reasonable privacy and confidentiality protections."

Page 3, line 3, strike "of personal data" and insert "to mitigate individuals' privacy risks."

Page 3, line 7, P3; L7: insert "analyzing," after "sharing."

Page 3, after line 21, insert the following (and re- designate subsequent paragraphs accordingly):

(6) multidisciplinary socio-technical research that fosters broader understanding of privacy preferences, requirements, and human behavior to in form the design and adoption of effective privacy solutions;

Page 5, lines 8 through 11, strike "to create and disseminate voluntary, technical standards, best practices, and guidelines, methodologies, procedures, and processes to cost-effectively ensure" and insert "to inform the development and dissemination of voluntary, consensus-based technical standards, guidelines, methodologies, procedures, and processes to cost-effectively increase."

Page 6, line 16, insert "and adoption" after "implementation."

Chairwoman JOHNSON. I ask unanimous consent to dispense with the reading. Without objection, so ordered. I now recognize the gentlelady for 5 minutes to explain that amendment, the second amendment.

Ms. STEVENS. Yes. Thank you, Madam Chair.

In explanation of the second amendment, we are making technical corrections to the definition of privacy-enhancing technologies, particularly to align with the NIST privacy framework. And this updated definition will capture more PETs and allow NIST and NSF to better follow the science. This change also—and along with striking the definition for personal data—changes the focus of the bill from protecting data to mitigating privacy risks and preventing check-the-box privacy compliance. We must encourage organizations to think critically about how they are protecting individuals' privacy and ensure that they have the tools to do so.

The amendment also adds a provision to the research activities outlined in the NSF section to support sociotechnical research that fosters broader understanding of privacy preferences and requirements and human behavior. This type of research will be essential to inform the design and facilitate the adoption of effective PETs.

Finally, the amendment ensures that the report requires under section 6 offering recommendations to Congress on how to boost the Federal adoption of this technology. It's exciting. I encourage and urge my colleagues to support this commonsense amendment to enhance and further improve the definition—definitions and PET research activities authorized in this bill. Thank you, and I yield back.

Chairwoman JOHNSON. Well, thank you. Any further discussion?

If there is no further discussion, the vote occurs on the amendment.

All those in favor, say aye.

Those opposed, say no.

The ayes have it, and the amendment is agreed to.

A Member may request a roll call vote, but I think we passed it.

The next amendment on the roster is an amendment offered by the gentleman from Florida, Mr. Posey. And you're recognized for 5 minutes.

Mr. POSEY. Thank you, Madam Chair. I have an amendment at the desk.

Chairwoman JOHNSON. The Clerk will report the amendment.

The CLERK. Amendment No. 3, amendment to the amendment in the nature of a substitute to H.R.——

[The amendment of Mr. Posey follows:]

Amendment to the Amendment in the Nature of a Substitute to H.R. 847 Offered by Mr. Posey of Florida

Add at the end the following:

Sec. 7. Protecting Personal Identifying Information

Any personal identifying information collected or stored through the activities authorized in this Act shall be done in accordance with section 690 of title 45, Code of Federal Regulations (relating to the protection of human subjects), or any successor regulation.

> Chairwoman JOHNSON. I ask unanimous consent to dispense with the reading. Without objection, so ordered.
> I recognize the gentleman for 5 minutes to explain his amendment.
> Mr. POSEY. Thank you, Chairwoman Johnson.
> My amendment would ensure that any collection or storage of personally identifiable information as part of the activities authorized in this act shall be done in consistency with the Common Rule or any subsequent Federal regulation. This Federal regulation ensures that if any personal data is collected and utilized through this work, it will require informed consent from the individual before it may be used.
> As has been mentioned already, harnessing the power of data will be a critical tool to unlocking the full potential of advanced technologies of artificial intelligence, but as we develop these emerging technologies, we must also protect our shared values of privacy, accountability, and transparency. This amendment ensures that we do just that, and I urge support and yield back the balance of my time.
> Chairwoman JOHNSON. Thank you. I now recognize myself to speak on this amendment.
> I thank Representative Posey for his amendment. It ensures that research conducted to improve the PETs does not create a privacy problem itself. I agree with Mr. Posey that all research that deals with human subjects should follow the Common Rule. I support this good amendment, and I yield back the balance of my time.
> Anyone else seeking time?
> If there's no discussion—further discussion on the amendment, the vote occurs on the amendment.
> All in favor, say aye.
> Those opposed, no.
> The ayes have it, and the amendment is agreed to.
> Now, we will vote on the amendment in the nature of a substitute, as amended. The vote occurs on the amendment.
> All those in favor, say aye.
> Those opposed, say no.
> The ayes have it, and the amendment is agreed to.
> Having a reporting quorum being present, I move that the Committee on Science, Space, and Technology report H.R. 847, as amended, to the House with the recommendation that the bill be approved.
> Those in favor of the motion will signify by saying aye.
> Those opposed, no.
> The ayes have it, and the bill is favorably reported.
> Without objection, the motion to reconsider is laid upon the table. I ask unanimous consent that the staff be authorized to make any necessary technical and conforming changes to the bill. Without objection, so ordered.
> Members will have 2 subsequent calendar days in which to submit supplemental, minority, or additional views on this measure.

Chapter 3

Deep Fakes and National Security[*]

Kelley M. Sayler and Laurie A. Harris

"Deep fakes"—a term that first emerged in 2017 to describe realistic photo, audio, video, and other forgeries generated with artificial intelligence (AI) technologies—could present a variety of national security challenges in the years to come. As these technologies continue to mature, they could hold significant implications for congressional oversight, U.S. defense authorizations and appropriations, and the regulation of social media platforms.

How Are Deep Fakes Created?

Though definitions vary, deep fakes are most commonly described as forgeries created using techniques in machine learning (ML)—a subfield of AI—especially generative adversarial networks (GANs). In the GAN process, two ML systems called neural networks are trained in competition with each other. The first network, or the generator, is tasked with creating counterfeit data—such as photos, audio recordings, or video footage—that replicate the properties of the original data set. The second network, or the discriminator, is tasked with identifying the counterfeit data. Based on the results of each iteration, the generator network adjusts to create increasingly realistic data. The networks continue to compete—often for thousands or millions of

---

[*] This is an edited, reformatted and augmented version of Congressional Research Service Publication No. IF11333, updated June 3, 2022.

In: Digital Identification
Editor: Lottie Gould
ISBN: 979-8-89113-494-2
© 2024 Nova Science Publishers, Inc.

iterations—until the generator improves its performance such that the discriminator can no longer distinguish between real and counterfeit data.

Though media manipulation is not a new phenomenon, the use of AI to generate deep fakes is causing concern because the results are increasingly realistic, rapidly created, and cheaply made with freely available software and the ability to rent processing power through cloud computing. Thus, even unskilled operators could download the requisite software tools and, using publically available data, create increasingly convincing counterfeit content.

How Could Deep Fakes Be Used?

Deep fake technology has been popularized for entertainment purposes—for example, social media users inserting the actor Nicholas Cage into movies in which he did not originally appear and a museum generating an interactive exhibit with artist Salvador Dalí. Deep fake technologies have also been used for beneficial purposes. For example, medical researchers have reported using GANs to synthesize fake medical images to train disease detection algorithms for rare diseases and to minimize patient privacy concerns.

Deep fakes could, however, be used for nefarious purposes. State adversaries or politically motivated individuals could release falsified videos of elected officials or other public figures making incendiary comments or behaving inappropriately. Doing so could, in turn, erode public trust, negatively affect public discourse, or even sway an election.

Indeed, the U.S. intelligence community concluded that Russia engaged in extensive influence operations during the 2016 presidential election to "undermine public faith in the U.S. democratic process, denigrate Secretary Clinton, and harm her electability and potential presidency." Likewise, in March 2022, Ukrainian President Volodymyr Zelensky announced that a video posted to social media—in which he appeared to direct Ukrainian soldiers to surrender to Russian forces—was a deep fake. While experts noted that this deep fake was not particularly sophisticated, in the future, convincing audio or video forgeries could potentially strengthen malicious influence operations.

Deep fakes could also be used to embarrass or blackmail elected officials or individuals with access to classified information. Already there is evidence that foreign intelligence operatives have used deep fake photos to create fake social media accounts from which they have attempted to recruit sources. Some analysts have suggested that deep fakes could similarly be used to generate inflammatory content—such as convincing video of U.S. military personnel engaged in war crimes—intended to radicalize populations, recruit terrorists, or incite violence. Section 589F of the FY2021 National Defense Authorization Act (P.L. 116-283) directs the Secretary of Defense to conduct an intelligence assessment of the threat posed by deep fakes to servicemembers and their families, including an assessment of the maturity of the technology and how it might be used to conduct information operations.

In addition, deep fakes could produce an effect that professors Danielle Keats Citron and Robert Chesney have termed the "Liar's Dividend"; it involves the notion that individuals could successfully deny the authenticity of genuine content—particularly if it depicts inappropriate or criminal behavior—by claiming that the content is a deep fake. Citron and Chesney suggest that the Liar's Dividend could become more powerful as deep fake technology proliferates and public knowledge of the technology grows.

Some reports indicate that such tactics have already been used for political purposes. For example, political opponents of Gabon President Ali Bongo asserted that a video intended to demonstrate his good health and mental competency was a deep fake, later citing it as part of the justification for an attempted coup. Outside experts were unable to determine the video's authenticity, but one expert noted, "in some ways it doesn't matter if [the video is] a fake... It can be used to just undermine credibility and cast doubt."

How Can Deep Fakes Be Detected?

Today, deep fakes can often be detected without specialized detection tools. However, the sophistication of the technology is rapidly progressing to a point at which unaided human detection will be very difficult or impossible. While commercial industry has been investing in automated deep fake detection tools, this section describes U.S. government investments and activities.

The Identifying Outputs of Generative Adversarial Networks Act (P.L. 116-258) directed NSF and NIST to support research on GANs. Specifically, NSF is directed to support research on manipulated or synthesized content and information authenticity, and NIST is directed to support research for the development of measurements and standards necessary to develop tools to examine the function and outputs of GANs or other technologies that synthesize or manipulate content.

In addition, DARPA has had two programs devoted to the detection of deep fakes: Media Forensics (MediFor) and Semantic Forensics (SemaFor).

MediFor, which concluded in FY2021, was to develop algorithms to automatically assess the integrity of photos and videos and to provide analysts with information about how counterfeit content was generated. The program reportedly explored techniques for identifying the audio-visual inconsistencies present in deep fakes, including inconsistencies in pixels (digital integrity), inconsistencies with the laws of physics (physical integrity), and inconsistencies with other information sources (semantic integrity). MediFor technologies are expected to transition to operational commands and the intelligence community.

SemaFor seeks to build upon MediFor technologies and to develop algorithms that will automatically detect, attribute, and characterize (i.e., identify as either benign or malicious) various types of deep fakes. This program is to catalog semantic inconsistencies—such as the mismatched earrings seen in the GAN-generated image in Figure 1, or unusual facial features or backgrounds—and prioritize suspected deep fakes for human review. DARPA requested $28.9 million for SemaFor in FY2023, $7.9 million above the FY2022 appropriation. Technologies developed by both SemaFor and MediFor are intended to improve defenses against adversary information operations.

Source: https://www.darpa.mil/news-events/2019-09-03a.

Figure 1. Example of Semantic Inconsistency in a GAN-Generated Image.

Policy Considerations

Some analysts have noted that algorithm-based detection tools could lead to a cat-and-mouse game, in which the deep fake generators are rapidly updated to address flaws identified by detection tools. For this reason, they argue that social media platforms—in addition to deploying deep fake detection tools—may need to expand the means of labeling and/or authenticating content. This could include a requirement that users identify the time and location at which the content originated or that they label edited content as such.

Other analysts have expressed concern that regulation of deep fake technology could impose undue burden on social media platforms or lead to unconstitutional restrictions on free speech and artistic expression. These analysts have suggested that existing law is sufficient for managing the malicious use of deep fakes. Some experts have asserted that responding with technical tools alone will be insufficient and that instead the focus should be on the need to educate the public about deep fakes and minimize incentives for creators of malicious deep fakes.

Potential Questions for Congress

- Do the Department of Defense, the Department of State, and the intelligence community have adequate information about the state of foreign deep fake technology and the ways in which this technology may be used to harm U.S. national security?
- How mature are DARPA's efforts to develop automated deep fake detection tools? What are the limitations of DARPA's approach, and are any additional efforts required to ensure that malicious deep fakes do not harm U.S. national security?
- Are federal investments and coordination efforts, across defense and nondefense agencies and with the private sector, adequate to address research and development needs and national security concerns regarding deep fake technologies?
- How should national security considerations with regard to deep fakes be balanced with free speech protections, artistic expression, and beneficial uses of the underlying technologies?
- Should social media platforms be required to authenticate or label content? Should users be required to submit information about the

provenance of content? What secondary effects could this have for social media platforms and the safety, security, and privacy of users?
- To what extent and in what manner, if at all, should social media platforms and users be held accountable for the dissemination and impacts of malicious deep fake content?
- What efforts, if any, should the U.S. government undertake to ensure that the public is educated about deep fakes?

CRS Products

CRS Report R45178, Artificial Intelligence and National Security, by Kelley M. Sayler

CRS Report R46795, Artificial Intelligence: Background, Selected Issues, and Policy Considerations, by Laurie A. Harris

CRS Report R45142, Information Warfare: Issues for Congress, by Catherine A. Theohary

Chapter 4

Science and Tech Spotlight: Deepfakes*

United States Government Accountability Office

Why This Matters

Deepfakes are powerful tools that can be used for exploitation and disinformation. Deepfakes could influence elections and erode trust but so far have mainly been used for non-consensual pornography. The underlying artificial intelligence (AI) technologies are widely available at low cost, and improvements are making deepfakes harder to detect.

The Technology

What is it? A deepfake is a video, photo, or audio recording that seems real but has been manipulated with AI. The underlying technology can replace faces, manipulate facial expressions, synthesize faces, and synthesize speech. Deepfakes can depict someone appearing to say or do something that they in fact never said or did.

While deepfakes have benign and legitimate applications in areas such as entertainment and commerce, they are commonly used for exploitation.

---

* This is an edited, reformatted and augmented version of the United States Government Accountability Office, Science, Technology Assessment, and Analytics Publication No. GAO-20-379SP, dated February 2020.

In: Digital Identification
Editor: Lottie Gould
ISBN: 979-8-89113-494-2
© 2024 Nova Science Publishers, Inc.

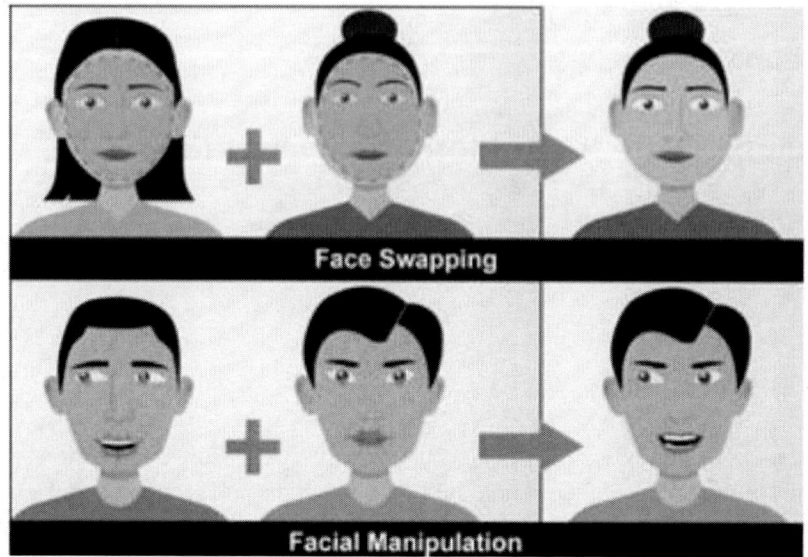
Source: GAO | GAO-20-379SP.

Figure 1. Deepfake videos commonly swap faces or manipulate facial expressions. In face swapping, the face on the left is placed on another person's body. In facial manipulation, the expressions of the face on the left are imitated by the face on the right.

According to a recent report from the company Deeptrace, much of deepfake content online is pornographic, and deepfake pornography disproportionately victimizes women. Further, there is concern about potential growth in the use of deepfakes for other purposes, particularly disinformation. Deepfakes could be used to influence elections or incite civil unrest, or as a weapon of psychological warfare. They could also lead to disregard of legitimate evidence of wrongdoing and, more generally, undermine public trust in audiovisual content.

How does it work? Deepfakes rely on artificial neural networks, which are computer systems modeled loosely on the human brain that recognize patterns in data. Developing a deepfake photo or video typically involves feeding hundreds or thousands of images into the artificial neural network, "training" it to identify and reconstruct patterns—usually faces.

Deepfakes use different underlying AI technologies—notably autoencoders and generative adversarial networks (GANs). An autoencoder is an artificial neural network trained to reconstruct input from a simpler representation. A GAN is made up of two competing artificial neural networks, one trying to produce a fake, the other trying to detect it. This competition continues over many cycles, resulting in a more plausible rendering of, for example, faces in video. GANs generally produce more convincing deepfakes but are more difficult to use.

Researchers and internet companies have experimented with several methods to detect deepfakes. These methods typically also use AI to analyze videos for digital artifacts or details that deepfakes fail to imitate realistically, such as blinking or facial tics.

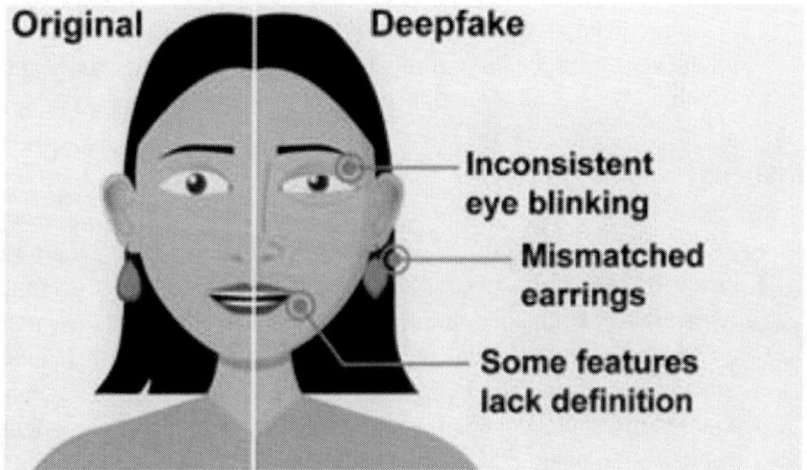

Source: GAO; conceived from DARPA image at http://www.darpa.mil/news-events2019-09-03a. | GAO-20-379SP.

Figure 2. Examples of characteristics that may indicate a deepfake.

How mature is it? Anyone with basic computer skills and a home computer can create a deepfake. Computer applications are openly available on the internet with tutorials on how to create deepfake videos. However, to develop a somewhat realistic deepfake, these applications generally still require hundreds or thousands of training images of the faces to be swapped or manipulated, making celebrities and government leaders the most common subjects. More convincing deepfakes created with GANs require more advanced technical skills and resources. As artificial neural network technologies have advanced rapidly in parallel with more powerful and abundant computing, so has the ability to produce realistic deepfakes.

Opportunities

There are some potentially benign or beneficial uses of this technology:

- Entertainment. Voices and likenesses can be used in a movie to achieve a creative effect or maintain a cohesive story when the entertainers themselves are not available.
- E-commerce. Retailers could let customers use their likenesses to virtually try on clothing.
- Communication. Speech synthesis and facial manipulation can make it appear that a person is authentically speaking another language.

Challenges

- Data needs for detection. Deepfake detection tools must generally be trained with large and diverse data sets to reliably detect deepfakes. Technology companies and researchers have released data sets to help train detection tools, but the current data sets are not sufficient by themselves. Detection tools must be constantly updated with data of increasing sophistication to ensure that they continue to be effective at detecting manipulated media.
- Detection is not yet automated. Current tools cannot perform a complete and automated analysis that reliably detects deepfakes. Research programs are currently working on means to automatically detect deepfakes, provide information on how they were created, and assess the overall integrity of digital content.
- Adaptation to detection. Techniques used to identify deepfakes tend to lead to the development of more sophisticated deepfake techniques. This "cat and mouse" situation means detection tools must be regularly updated to keep pace.
- Detection may not be enough. Even a perfect detection technology may not prevent a fake video from being effective as disinformation, because many viewers may be unaware of deepfakes or may not take the time to check the reliability of the videos they see.
- Inconsistent social media standards. The major social media companies have different standards for moderating deepfakes.

- Legal issues. Proposed laws or regulations addressing deepfake media may raise questions regarding an individual's freedom of speech and expression and the privacy rights of individuals falsely portrayed in deepfakes. Moreover, potential federal legislation aimed at combating deepfakes could face enforcement challenges.

Policy Context and Questions

Any policy response seeking to address deepfakes would likely face constitutional and other legal challenges along with the technical challenges of detection. Key policy questions include:

- What is the maturity of deepfake detection technology? How much progress have federal programs and public-private partnerships made in developing such technology? What expertise will be required to ensure detection keeps pace with deepfake technology?
- What rights do individuals have to their privacy and likenesses? What rights do creators of deepfakes have under the First Amendment? What policy options exist regarding election interference? What policy options exist regarding exploitation and image abuse, such as non-consensual pornography?
- What can be done to educate the public about deepfakes? Should manipulated media be marked or labeled? Should media be traceable to its origin to determine authenticity?
- What should the roles of media outlets and social media companies be in detecting and moderating content that has been altered or falsified?

Selected GAO Work

- Technology Assessment: Artificial Intelligence: Emerging Opportunities, Challenges, and Implications, GAO-18-142SP.

Selected References

Ajder, Henry et al. The State of Deepfakes: Landscape, Threats, and Impact. Amsterdam, Netherlands: Deeptrace, 2019.

Barrett, Paul M. Disinformation and the 2020 Election: How the Social Media Industry Should Prepare. New York, N.Y.: NYU Stern Center for Business and Human Rights, 2019.

Centre for Data Ethics and Innovation. Deepfakes and Audio-visual Disinformation. London, United Kingdom: 2019.

Collins, Aengus. Forged Authenticity: Governing Deepfake Risks. Lausanne, Switzerland: EPFL International Risk Governance Center, 2019.

Library of Congress. Congressional Research Service. Deep Fakes and National Security. IF11333. Washington, D.C.: Oct. 14, 2019.

Westerlund, Mika. "The Emergence of Deepfake Technology: A Review." Technology Innovation Management Review, vol. 9, no. 11 (2019): pp. 39-52.

Gao Support

GAO meets congressional information needs in several ways, including by providing oversight, insight, and foresight on science and technology issues. GAO staff are available to brief on completed bodies of work or specific reports and answer follow-up questions. GAO also provides targeted assistance on specific science and technology topics to support congressional oversight activities and provide advice on legislative proposals.

Timothy M. Persons, PhD, Chief Scientist, personst@gao.gov

Staff Acknowledgments

Karen Howard (Director), Laura Holliday (Assistant Director), Sushil Sharma (Assistant Director), Chi Mai (Analyst-in-Charge), Adam Brooks (Analyst), Anika McMillon, and Ben Shouse.

This document is not an audit product and is subject to revision based on continued advances in science and technology. It contains information prepared by GAO to provide technical insight to legislative bodies or other external organizations. This document has been reviewed by the Chief Scientist of the U.S. Government Accountability Office.